Dining Etiquette Simplified

Christine Hunter-Carmichael

Christine Carmichael loves to meet and chat with fans! Reach out to her at ccarmichael@flemmingetiquette.com.

Edited by Chaya Braxton - chayLEVEL Content = Communications
Book Cover by Publishing Hackers

ISBN (Paperback): 978-1-959911-27-2

To my family and friends, whose unwavering support and love have always been my foundation. To my esteemed clients, whose eagerness to learn and commitment to personal growth inspire every page of this journey.

And to all those aspiring to refine their lives and manners— may this book light your way.

Contents

Welcome

Welcome to *Dining Etiquette Simplified*! I'm thrilled to guide you through the "Do's and Don'ts of dining etiquette" in a way that's practical, and completely do-able.

Our mission is to help you feel poised and confident at the table so you aren't worrying about "doing it right or wrong," you can enjoy the dining experience.

So why *Dining Etiquette Simplified*?

Dining etiquette doesn't have to be complicated—it's an art that anyone can master, regardless of their background.

As Henry Wadsworth Longfellow said, "In character, in manners, in style, in all things, the supreme excellence is simplicity."

Dining is not just about eating—it's presenting your best self at the table and creating memorable experiences.

Usually, when I walk into a room before I begin my in-person presentations, people seem a little nervous and uneasy. They sit up a little straighter and even raise their pinky finger when they pick up their utensils.

Do you feel the same way? Well don't worry!

Even though we are learning and sharpening our skills, this is a respectful and safe space. Think of this as your personal classroom and I'm your coach.

Soooo, take a deep breath and let's begin!

Congratulations on your decision to refine you and the way you show up!

Preface

In today's fast-paced world, the grace and elegance of traditional dining are often overshadowed by our hectic schedules. Let's face it, many of us don't have the time to sit down for a proper dinner anymore. It is quicker to microwave a meal or race through a drive-through before or after work or after karate practice with the kids. Yet, I want to submit to you that dining etiquette remains a timeless art—one that not only elevates our dining experiences but also reminds us to honor ourselves and those around us. After all, when you carry yourself with dignity and respect, you are, in essence, respecting your royalty.

This book stems from my firm belief that dining etiquette is more than just following rules. Etiquette can improve the quality of our interactions with people, bringing deeper meaning to our experiences to create a strong tight-knit, authentic community

My journey into the world of etiquette began years ago when a good friend and I recognized a need within our community. I began to tell her about a series of events that happened while I was running errands.

One hot summer day, I was coming out of the market when I saw an older woman struggling with her groceries, trying to get them into her car. Just a few feet away, a young guy was strolling by with his friends, laughing and talking rather loudly.

door; I saw a young lady rush ahead of an older man, with a visible impediment, who was also going inside. She went right in without holding the door for him or even acknowledging he was there.

These little moments might seem trivial, but they show a real lack of consideration and respect that's becoming too common. It's important to remember that simple acts of kindness and respect can make a big difference. Respecting others begins with respecting yourself. It's about showing up with intention, treating every interaction as an opportunity to uplift those around you—and that starts with embracing your own sense of royalty. As I complained to my dear friend Sherry, she began to list activities that would build character and add value to their lives. "And a little etiquette would be helpful!" she said. We both recounted how at different times in our own lives we struggled to speak up and show up with confidence. This realization sparked my passion for teaching etiquette, and we dedicated ourselves to equipping young people with the tools they need to navigate their everyday experiences with poise and self-assurance.

Growing up as a first-generation Jamaican Canadian, I learned early on that satisfying Granny's standards meant mastering more than just eating cornmeal porridge in my high chair. If I didn't meet her expectations, I faced a deep eye-roll and the most serious "chupse" that could move heaven and earth. Granny's rules were clear: no sitting on her bed in street clothes, dresses required stockings and slips, meals were strictly in the kitchen, and lounging with crossed legs in front of the TV was  a no-go. Let's not forget, speaking out of turn was unthinkable; Granny expected silence unless spoken to. At the time, it felt unjust, but these experiences taught me invaluable lessons in boundaries, flexibility, and the dreaded "D" word: discipline. As an etiquette consultant and motivational speaker, I've come to appreciate that there's often a better way of doing things, if we remain open to growth and learning. The wisdom of the late Dr. Myles Munroe continually inspires me to seek that better way by understanding our purpose and the purpose of "things" in our lives. He insightfully reminds us, "where purpose is not known, abuse is inevitable." This guidance encourages me to approach each endeavor with clarity and intention, elevating even the simplest actions into opportunities for excellence. Those early lessons continue to shape how I approach life and help others navigate their own paths with grace and respect.

Later in my career, I had the privilege of working at the esteemed Jefferson Hotel in Richmond, Virginia—a Four Diamond property known for its luxurious comfort, grandeur, and elegance. During my time there, paying attention to details and anticipating guests' needs were an important part of my job.

I learned important lessons that continue to shape my life's work.

Every Sunday morning, guests and locals would gather eagerly in the mezzanine on the second floor and the rotunda on the first, brimming with anticipation for our lavish, beautifully curated brunch. It was a feast for the senses, a celebration of flavors and presentation, crafted to delight to indulge each guest.

Each week, we had all types of guests—wealthy and affluent regulars, excited newlyweds, and families who had saved up just to be there. I noticed how our warm hospitality and elegant atmosphere made everyone feel special, no matter who they were. It reminded me that true etiquette is all about making everyone feel valued and appreciated, no matter their background.

Something resonated in my heart. It occurred to me that I could help others access these types of experiences by teaching them etiquette. It's about granting access to luxury, elegance, and grandeur to everyone regardless of their background or circumstances. Our hospitality ensured that all individuals have the opportunity to enjoy and feel valued in spaces traditionally associated with privilege. It's about creating environments where every guest feels welcomed, respected, and able to indulge in the finest available. This commitment to accessibility in bodacious hospitality enriches experiences and strengthens the fabric of our communities.

My passion for etiquette grew as I realized its power to transform ordinary moments into extraordinary encounters. This book is a culmination of my experiences, insights, and dedication to the art of dining in western culture. It is designed to be a comprehensive guide that covers both the fundamental principles of etiquette and the subtleties that can elevate a dining experience from good to exceptional.

I'll be honest—when I first sat down to write this book, I wasn't sure if I should venture beyond western table manners. I mean, I didn't want my friends across the globe to feel left out, but covering every dining tradition would have required a lot more pages (and maybe a passport or two!). So, while the focus here is on western dining etiquette, I couldn't resist adding a small chapter on global practices. Think of this book as a little bonus tour around the world—no plane ticket required! These insights may just save you from an accidental faux pas at your next international dinner party.

As you read through these pages, I hope you find the joy and satisfaction that come from mastering table manners. We'll cover everything from navigating the table setting with finesse to hosting a successful dinner event so you can feel confident and serve effortlessly while enjoying your guests. The tips in this book will help you handle any dining situation with confidence and ease. Whether you're hosting a fancy dinner, attending a casual get-together, or sharing a meal with family and friends, this book will provide you with the knowledge and confidence to shine in any dining scenario.

Setting the Stage for Success

Where business deals unfold over dinner and romantic connections are kindled at cozy cafes, mastering dining etiquette is not merely an option; it's a necessity. Whether you're a young professional looking to climb the career ladder, someone who values refinement, or simply relishes elegance, this chapter is your foundational guide to understanding why dining etiquette matters and how it can be your ticket to success.

One of my followers on TikTok shared their dating fiasco: Gavin was excited for his first date with Alisa, a charming woman he met through mutual friends. They decided on a cozy, upscale restaurant known for its intimate ambiance and delicious cuisine. Gavin arrived early, eager to make a good impression.

When Alisa walked in, she looked stunning. Gavin stood up and pulled out her chair; they exchanged pleasantries and a hug. He felt very optimistic, "This is off to a great start," he thought. Everything was perfect—until the food arrived. As soon as their meals came, Alisa picked up her phone.

Gavin thought, "Okay, this is not unusual." She is just taking a picture of her entree!" To his disappointment, Alisa started scrolling through social media. Gavin tried to engage her in conversation, but she responded with distracted nods and one-word answers. He could not believe what he was witnessing as pangs of disappointment began to settle.

Midway through their meal, Alisa's phone rang. Instead of silencing it, she took the call, chatting loudly about her plans for the weekend, while Gavin sat there, awkwardly stirring his pasta. The tension in the air was thick, and the awkwardness of the situation was undeniable.

Things went from bad to worse when the dessert arrived. Alisa dug into her tiramisu with child-like excitement, talking with her mouth full. Gavin's face grew red with embarrassment as nearby diners shot them disapproving glances.

When the bill came, Gavin, like the gentleman he is, presented his card. Alisa didn't bat an eye or even thank Gavin. She grabbed her coat and announced, "Well, that was… interesting. Let's do it again sometime," as she gathered her phone and her purse. She stood up without waiting for him and proceeded to the door. The abruptness of her departure left Gavin standing there, stunned and speechless.

As he left the restaurant, he knew one thing for sure: there wouldn't be a second date. Bad etiquette had turned what could have been a pleasant evening into a regrettable experience.

Dining etiquette is not just a set of arbitrary rules; it's a powerful tool for creating lasting impressions. Think of it as your invitation into the refined circle of polished individuals who navigate any social or professional setting with ease and confidence. This is your inside track to becoming someone who moves gracefully, equipped with the poise and awareness that makes a lasting impression wherever you go. Mastering dining etiquette can help you secure that business deal, impress your date, or simply enjoy a meal without any social awkwardness.

Here's why dining etiquette is significant:

Making a positive impression

Dining etiquette helps you to present yourself in the best possible light. Good manners and table etiquette help create a positive impression and reputation.

Building relationships

Networking is the lifeblood of your career. Establishing connections and building meaningful relationships can open doors. Businesses are made up of people, so learning how to communicate effectively and authentically is crucial. When you demonstrate impeccable dining etiquette, you not only make a favorable impression but also convey respect for others, laying the foundation for future partnerships. In other words, dining etiquette is your secret weapon for networking success.

Sharing a meal is a social activity that provides an opportunity to connect with others. Learning and using proper dining etiquette can help build relationships with colleagues, clients, and others.

I have met the most incredible people around the dinner table. Over the last few years, I have developed a very meaningful relationship with Andre. He is a wildly creative and passionate interior designer. Andre attended one of my dining etiquette events, and we've been connected ever since. Andre isn't just any friend; he's the kind who publicly refers you to his clients at his own events. How many people are willing to go to those lengths? Thanks to his referral, I've had the opportunity to work alongside other amazing businesses. Since then, he has attended many of my classes, always learning and sharing his thoughts and lessons with everyone.

"I just learn something new every time we're together," he said.

I remember one dinner in particular where Andre's sense of humor was in full swing! We were at this fancy restaurant, and Andre decided it was time to educate the entire table on the "correct" way to eat spaghetti. With the precision of a surgeon and the theatrics of a Broadway actor, he twirled his fork and spoon with great flair. Just as he was about to take a bite, a stray noodle flew across the table and hit a fellow dinner guest square in the forehead. Without missing a beat, Andre exclaimed, "And that, ladies and gentlemen, is why you should always wear a bib to dinner!" The whole table erupted in laughter, and even the poor target of the noodle attack couldn't help but join in

Moments like these make dining with friends so memorable. Andre's humor and generosity have made our friendship very special.

Demonstrating respect

Dining etiquette is a way to show respect for others and cultural traditions. You can avoid unintentionally offending others by understanding and following proper dining etiquette.

Enhancing professionalism

Proper dining etiquette is often expected in business settings and can help you demonstrate your professionalism and attention to detail.

Reducing stress

Knowing and practicing proper dining etiquette can help you feel more confident and at ease in social situations, which reduces stress and anxiety. We want our table manners to become so effortless that our focus during the meal is on the people we are with rather than which fork to use. We believe that good manners are a courtesy to those with whom we eat.

In the heart of the bustling city of Montreal and after countless interviews, Deidre found herself on the precipice of a pivotal job interview. The position was for a prestigious marketing role at a renowned advertising agency, a job that could potentially change the course of her career and her life. Her knowledge and skills were impeccable; she had an impressive portfolio to back up her qualifications.

For weeks, she had meticulously prepared herself for this interview, researching the company, rehearsing her elevator pitch, and carefully selecting her interview attire. But as her interview date approached, the fear of a disastrous lunch interview grew stronger. She heard that potential employers often assessed how candidates carried themselves at the table to reflect their overall professionalism and social aptitude. And Deidre's dining etiquette left much to be desired.

In an upscale French bistro, where the interview was scheduled, Deidre arrived early. Her heart was racing. She couldn't afford to let a simple meal stand between her and her dream job. As she waited at the elegant table, she glanced around at the other diners, observing their impeccable manners. Everyone seemed so poised and confident that their cutlery looked like a natural extension of their hands.

Moments later, her prospective employer, Madame Giselle Fortin, a very classy woman in her mid-fifties, entered the restaurant and approached her table with a warm smile. Deidre rose to greet her, feeling a knot of anxiety tighten in her stomach. The savory aroma of the filet mignon and lobster bisque dishes filled the air as the waiter presented them with the menu. Deidre scanned it carefully, trying to appear composed and knowledgeable about fine dining.

The first hurdle came when the server presented the wine list. Deidre knew the importance of wine pairing, and her expertise was limited to choosing between red and white. On the other hand, Mme. Fortin appeared to be a connoisseur who seemed to know the extensive list by heart. Sweating slightly, she fumbled for words, stammering, "I think I'll have... a red wine, please."

Mme. Fortin raised an eyebrow, "Certainly, but with which specific wine would you prefer?"

Deidre felt her cheeks burn with embarrassment. She didn't want to come across as clueless, so she decided to take a shot in the dark, "I'll go with the Merlot."

The waiter nodded and disappeared to retrieve the wine, leaving Deidre anxiously second-guessing her choice.

As the meal progressed, the challenges of dining etiquette only grew. She tried to maintain a casual conversation with Mme. Fortin while juggling her fork and knife. Deidre attempted to cut the filet mignon gracefully. Despite her best efforts, she dropped the fork and spilled sauce on her pristine white napkin.

Deidre noticed Mme. Fortin's watchful eyes showed that her lack of dining etiquette had not gone unnoticed. "Good grief!" She cursed herself for not taking those etiquette classes more seriously.

The tension had become palpable as dessert was served, and Deidre was sure she had blown her chances. But to her surprise, Mme. Fortin leaned in and broke the ice: "You know, Deidre, I was in your shoes once, and I understand that interviews can be quite nerve-wracking, but dining etiquette can be learned. What matters more is your passion, drive, and ability to adapt and grow. Your qualifications and enthusiasm for this role are truly impressive."

Deidre felt a glimmer of hope and released a sigh of relief. The conversation shifted to her experiences and how her skill set would benefit the company. Mme. Fortin was genuinely interested in her ideas, and the formality of the dinner slowly dissolved.

Ultimately, the interview was not solely about her dining etiquette; it was about her potential and ability to adapt and learn. Deidre's passion for the job, knowledge, and resilience in the face of her shortcomings made a lasting impression. She walked out of the restaurant, feeling she had a real chance at the position and with a new-found determination to master the art of dining etiquette, no matter the outcome. This interview taught her that the best qualifications sometimes go beyond what's on paper.

The story's moral is that your knowledge and skills may be top-notch, but the lack of dining etiquette can overshadow your qualifications. Employers often assess how a candidate carries themselves at the table as a reflection of their professionalism and social aptitude.

How do we set the stage?

We often hear that first impressions are lasting impressions, which couldn't be more accurate than when dining. Before you utter a word, your table manners, posture, and behavior convey a wealth of information about you.

Let's explore the key aspects of creating a stellar impression:

Dressing the Part

"Life's too short to wear boring clothes."
~Cushnie et Ochs

A crucial component of dining etiquette begins with how you present yourself. You've heard the saying, "don't judge a book by its cover" but unfortunately most of us do! So dress appropriately for the occasion, and remember that being slightly overdressed is always preferable to being underdressed. Your attire sets the tone and or expectation for the entire dining experience.

Confidence and Poise

Confidence is the bedrock of dining etiquette. When you enter a restaurant or join a table, do so with a sense of confidence. Walk tall, make eye contact, and greet others warmly. Confidence is contagious and will put everyone at ease. If just the thought of walking into a room filled with people makes you nauseous, "practice" will be your best friend. You don't have to wait for an invitation; you can dine on your own and practice your new skills!

Seating Etiquette

Knowing where to sit can be confusing in some settings. As a general rule, wait for your host to guide you or lead your guests to their seats. The person of honor should sit with their back to the wall, giving them a clear view of the room.

Table Posture

Your posture is a silent statement of your confidence and respect. Sit up straight, but don't be rigid, keeping your elbows close to your body and your forearms at the table's edge or in your lap. Avoid slouching, hunching over your plate, or spreading your elbows wide.

Cell Phone Etiquette

This is an easy one - put your cell phones away! Our phones have become a part of us that trying to convince us to put it down, is like trying to wrangle a slice of apple from a squirrel at a picnic - nearly impossible. It's essential to strike a balance between staying connected and being in the moment. I get it, capturing that beautifully arranged dish is a modern-day ritual, and it's cool but there's no need for a branding photoshoot! So snap your pic and keep it brief. Here's another kicker, flipping your phone screen down doesn't get you off the hook. The real deal is putting that gadget away completely, out of sight and mind. Trust me, it's the only way to save your meal from becoming a digital photo studio!

Keep your phone silent or on vibrate so it doesn't serenade the entire restaurant. And if you absolutely must take a call, consider it your dramatic exit for the evening, graciously excusing yourself from the table. After all, no one wants to be upstaged by a buzzing pocket performer!

Introducing Yourself

Networking events still bring a mix of excitement and anxiety for me. As a seasoned Etiquette Consultant, I understand the crucial role of making a good first impression.

At a recent Chesterfield Chamber of Commerce event, I saw an opportunity to expand my network and find new clients.

The event took place at Bryant & Stratton, a local college. The room buzzed with professionals mingling, exchanging business cards, and sharing laughs. I spotted a group where I recognized a few familiar faces and joined. Armed with a confident smile, I walked over, ready to introduce myself.

"Hello, I'm Christine," I said, making eye contact with each person in the circle. Yet, just as I extended my hand to shake with a man on my left, someone accidentally bumped into me from behind, causing my drink to splash all over the man's crisp white shirt.

For a split second, time seemed to freeze as I placed my right hand over my heart. My eyes widened, and my ears started to burn. The group appeared to sustain a silence as the man looked down at his now soggy shirt. "Oh my goodness, I am so, so sorry!" Did I mention that I was donning my gold-plated name badge? "Christine Carmichael, The Flemming Academy of Etiquette & Protocol." Etiquette, huh?

Attempting to remain composed, the man smiled and said, "Well, I guess that's one way to break the ice!" His attempt at humor was a welcome relief, and soon, the tension turned into laughter.

As I desperately tried to salvage the situation, I quickly grabbed a handful of napkins from a nearby table and handed them to him. "Let me help you with that," I offered (though my mortification was evident).

The group members started to chuckle, and soon, we laughed. One of the women in the group patted me on the shoulder and said, "Christine, it's great to meet you! Don't worry; we've all had our share of awkward moments." Hmmm, yes, but I'm an etiquette consultant. Did I mention that I was donning my gold-plated name badge? "Christine Carmichael, The Flemming Academy of Etiquette & Protocol." Etiquette, huh?

Gradually, the laughter and the warmth of the group helped ease my embarrassment. The man with the wet shirt even joked, "Well, at least I won't forget your name now!"

Despite the rocky start, the incident turned into a fantastic conversation starter. As the evening went on, we shared more stories of networking blunders and laughed about the unpredictability of such events. That night, I made several valuable connections, proving that even the most mortifying mishaps can lead to positive outcomes and valuable connections.

Remember that introducing yourself at a networking event may go differently than planned. But a sincere apology, a bit of humor, and genuine kindness can turn even the most awkward situations into memorable and bonding experiences.

Engaging in Small Talk

Engaging in polite conversation is a skill that can greatly enhance your dining experience. Ask open-ended questions and practice listening attentively to others. Steer clear of controversial topics and always show respect for opinions differing from yours.

Gabby and Summer Classics Richmond

Here are a few examples of conversation starters in a casual or social setting:

- "Do you have any exciting travel plans coming up? I'm always looking for new destinations to explore."

- "What's your go-to stress reliever or hobby when you're not at work?"

- "Any recommendations for a good restaurant or fun activity in the city? I'm always up for trying new things."

And in a business setting or networking event:

- "What are the most exciting trends or innovations in *[specific industry]* right now?"

- "How do you balance your work and personal life, especially in a demanding industry like *[specific industry]*?"

- "When it comes to professional development, what books, podcasts, or resources have significantly impacted your career, and why?"

These kinds of questions encourage in-depth responses and can lead to meaningful discussions, helping you to connect more genuinely with the people you meet.

Remember, dining etiquette isn't about adhering to rigid rules but rather about showing respect and consideration for others while presenting your best self. Whether you're attending a high-stakes business dinner, a family celebration, or a romantic rendezvous, the principles of making a great first impression and projecting confidence are universal.

Why Is This Important?

Appropriate behavior eliminates distractions! So, who dictates appropriate behavior? Society.

Etiquette is a code of polite behavior and conduct among members of a particular profession or group. Here are a few examples of inappropriate behavior that causes distractions:

- Talking on your phone during the movies or checking your socials because the light on your phone distracts the other moviegoers in a dark room

- Tailgating the car in front of you

- Speaking while others are presenting

- Snapping fingers or waving to get the server's attention

- If you're at a restaurant and see someone you know, saying hello is appropriate, but an entire discourse is inappropriate.

These are just a few distractions that we can change with a bit of etiquette and consideration.

Most of us have had positive experiences with food, haven't we? The different aromas of food can evoke both happy and sad memories. For instance, the scent of peaches may remind you of Granny's old-fashioned peach cobbler, bringing back cherished memories despite her passing. On the other hand, the smell of burnt toast may trigger memories of your first apartment—that tiny, barely affordable studio where you first ventured into independent living. The toaster, a thrift store find, never quite worked right, resulting in many mornings filled with trial and error and the smell of burnt toast. This aroma, mixed with the scent of fresh coffee, symbolized both your independence and the learning curve of living on your own.

Food not only provides the necessary nutrients for our bodies, but it also offers comfort. After a tiring day filled with meetings, studying, and a demanding schedule, we often seek out something that makes us feel good.

For me, that something includes the five-layer yellow batter chocolate iced cake lovingly made by Ukrop's Homestyle Foods. I usually place it in the microwave for about 15 seconds until the cake is slightly warm and the icing softens to a slow melt. Hmm, can you taste it? I think it's safe to say that food nourishes both our bodies and souls!

It's important for us that our food not only tastes good but also looks good. In all honesty, if our food doesn't look appealing, do we even want to try it?

Presentation is important. It drives our curiosity to know more..." Hmmm, this looks good; let me try it!" If it looks good, it must taste good, right? Well, not always. It may be overcooked, undercooked, or worse, just bland, but you get my point!

Good Food

Good food is better with the company of others! Some of my most enjoyable moments were sharing a meal. To be clear, this excluded those early days when my children were younger. I felt more like a referee calling plays and deciding penalties. "Mom, he's laughing at me!" or "Mom, she took the last piece of chicken!" or "I don't like the lemonade and sweet tea mixed together; you said that I can have the watermelon one?" How about this, "No get outttt, that's my seat!" Well by the time I sat down to dine, my meal was cold or tepid at best. These days, I enjoy sharing a meal with others just as much as dining alone.

What's Wrong With The Way I Eat?

Perhaps nothing! This point may be less important to you, your immediate family, or your circle of friends. For many of us, our home is our safe space for relaxation and letting our hair down. It's not a matter of "if" but "when" you're in an environment that benefits you to put your best foot forward, you can do so effortlessly and with confidence.

During my early days at a corporate Christmas party, I found myself seated next to a young executive who was determined to impress our President and the leadership team. When the lobster course arrived, he confidently picked up his knife and fork, ready to tackle the dish. Unfortunately, his lack of experience quickly became apparent.

He wrestled with the lobster like it was a stubborn child refusing to go to bed, sending pieces flying in every direction. The table tried to stifle their laughter, but it was impossible. The poor guy turned bright red, looking like he'd just fought a losing battle with a plate of live fireworks!

It was a hilarious yet stark reminder that knowing how to handle different foods can prevent embarrassing situations and allow you to enjoy the meal confidently.

Believe It or Not

I read that according to a Carnegie Report, up to 85% of your career success may be a result of your interpersonal skills. These skills not only determine your ability to present yourself and ideas effectively to people, but also have the potential to shape your professional journey. That client potentially may have questions like "will you work best with me" or "with my clients and my staff" or "mesh well with the culture of the organization". The purpose of a professional dining meal is the relationship you are creating, maintaining or enhancing. This insight should inspire you to invest in your personal growth and development of these crucial skills.

Connections

I know it seems counterintuitive to hope for a viable connection in an environment where you don't know anyone, but let me share what not to do!

I was excited about attending the "Going from Good to GREAT!!!" Small Business Conference at Virginia State University, sponsored by the Virginia Department of SBSD. Upon arrival, we received a warm welcome and the option to network with others during a complimentary continental breakfast.

I approached a table with three people and asked if I could join them. They eagerly agreed, so I waited until they finished their conversation and then introduced myself. A few minutes later, another gentleman joined us, and we moved into the usual icebreakers.

Then, bustling in came a lady with her hands full with a briefcase, purse, and a bag. She asked if she could sit at our table, everyone nodded while saying, "Of course!" As soon as she sat down, she pulled out her business cards and started handing them out like an elementary school teacher passing out graded tests. She barely made eye contact and didn't wait for each individual to respond before moving to the next person.

I could feel the energy shift at the table. Some were caught off guard because they were already engaged in other conversations, while others seemed confused. I'm sure we all thought to ourselves, "Who is this person?"

You will attend many events like this where you will meet new people. I know you can't wait to dazzle the room with your effervescent personality, but I want you to resist the urge to meet as many people as possible.

Bob Beaudine authored a book, "The Power of Who." It revolves around the idea that relationships and connections are the most important factors in achieving personal and professional success. The book's premise is centered on the "WHO," emphasizing the significance of the people we already know and the relationships we cultivate in realizing our goals and dreams.

Beaudine suggests that opportunities often arise through personal connections, referrals, and recommendations from the people within our network. For me, this takes the stress out of trying to meet everyone. So I don't have to pass out my business cards like I'm at a blackjack table. "You get a card, She gets a card, He gets a card, EVERYBODY gets a card!" If you're unfamiliar with this statement, google Oprah Winfrey's incredible car give-away. In 2004, Oprah gave everyone in her studio audience (approx. 276 people) a Pontiac G6. Most likely you won't get that kind of response to your service or product (you're still valuable to your niche market) but you don't need to. Instead, nurture those genuine connections—because Oprah-level hype isn't in the budget, and nobody's walking away with a free car from your meeting.

Mr. Beaudine encourages readers to identify and leverage their existing relationships to advance their careers, find fulfilling opportunities, and achieve their aspirations.

It is highly probable that you already know someone who knows someone who can assist you in your personal or professional goals, so don't worry or stress about meeting everyone in the room.

Dining Etiquette in the Digital Age

With so many "SMART" items, like appliances, TVs and coffeemakers; is it still smart to pull out your phone to call or text at the dinner table? Let's talk about the balance between the two and explore the art of sharing food experiences on social media, and mastering the fine art of texting and calling during meals.

The Device-Free Dining Rule

As you can imagine, this is a challenging exercise for everyone! Even though I ask my students to put their phones away during our dining etiquette workshop, they always seem to find their way back into their eager hands under the table.

So here's an idea!

Consider implementing a device-free dining rule for specific meals, where everyone agrees to put their phones away. This rule helps to encourage meaningful conversations and undistracted dining. Instead of incessantly checking your phone, use mealtime to truly engage with your dining companions.

In one of my friend groups, the rule is that if you pull out your cell phone, you pick up the tab—for everyone's entrée, which can be, "Très cher!"

Perhaps you can try this:

At a cozy neighborhood bistro, one of our etiquette consultants observed a group of friends dining together. Their phones became increasingly tempting as the meal progressed, leading to distracted conversations and interruptions. Realizing the need for a digital detox, one of the friends initiated a game - the "Phone Stack." Each person placed their phone in a stack in the center of the table. The first person to check their phone during the meal would have to cover the dessert. The result was an evening filled with laughter, meaningful conversations, and dessert-covered expenses.

Mindful Notifications

If you can't avoid checking your phone during a meal, put it on silent mode and manage notifications. Family emergencies or important work issues might necessitate a response, but personal and casual texts can generally wait.

Briefly excuse yourself from the table to respond to urgent messages, ensuring you maintain the flow of the meal. Whatever you do, do not engage in a lengthy phone conversation while dining with others. It sends the message that your conversation or the person at the end of the line is more important than the one in front of you.

Sharing Food Experiences on Social Media

Today dining is a sensory and visual experience, with many people eager to document their culinary adventures on social media. Here's how to do it tastefully:

1. *Ask for Permission:* Always ask your dining companions for permission before taking photos or posting about your meal. Respect their privacy and preferences.

2. *The Art of Discretion:* While capturing your dining experience, be discreet and avoid using flash photography in dimly lit restaurants. It's essential to consider the comfort of others.

3. *Posting:* If you intend to share your experience on social media, you might consider posting afterward. It doesn't take a long time to post but you want to avoid spending excessive time on your phone during the meal. Also do you want everyone to know where you are at that time?

Today, dining etiquette requires finesse and a little mindfulness. Balancing all of our devices, sharing food experiences on social media, and managing texts and calls are important skills to master.

Navigating Formal and Informal Dining Scenarios

At an elaborate, black-tie gala hosted by a prestigious international organization. My responsibility was to ensure that everyone, regardless of the event's poshness, felt at ease. I found myself in a very critical role. The event, a dazzling spectacle of luxury, was attended by individuals from diverse cultural backgrounds.

While mingling with the guests, I met a young woman named Emily. She was an up-and-coming executive, poised and accomplished, but she confessed to feeling lost in the sea of ornate cutlery, crystal glasses, and intimidating place settings. "I'm accustomed to more casual dining," she admitted, her eyes darting around the table in a mild panic.

Our task for the evening was to navigate a seven-course meal, complete with a symphony of silverware, wine pairings, and the intricacies of fine dining. The event's formality, with its array of utensils and dining etiquette rules, was a source of anxiety for many guests.

The evening was not without its share of mishaps—forks clattered to the floor, glasses teetered on the edge, and there was a moment when Emily's dinner roll took flight. Yet, we found that navigating formal dining scenarios through laughter and shared learning could be an enjoyable and enriching experience.

In this chapter, we will explore the art of handling both formal and informal dining scenarios with grace and ease.

Formal dining scenarios often demand a higher level of etiquette, which can feel overwhelming. This is a common idea, especially for those who are more accustomed to casual dining settings.

Here's a few tips to be mindful of:

Engaging in Table Conversation

In formal settings, engage in polite conversation with those around you. Avoid contentious and controversial topics and be a good listener. Allow the host or hostess to guide the conversation.

Elegant Posture

Maintain good posture and sit up straight, but not rigid. This reflects your confidence and respect for the event's formality. Good posture is a subtle yet powerful aspect of professional etiquette. It reflects confidence, respect, and attentiveness. Think about the example of Former First Lady, Michelle Obama. She is admired worldwide for her poise and posture. Whether she is delivering a speech, attending a formal event, or engaging with the public, Lady Michelle Obama consistently maintains an upright yet relaxed posture. Her shoulders are back, her head is held high, and she sits or stands with a sense of ease and grace. This not only enhances her presence but also conveys a message of self-assurance and respect for those around her. We feel comfortable with her. Let's talk about Kate Middleton, the Duchess of Cambridge,who is also known for her amazing posture. She always stands and sits with her back straight, shoulders back, and head held high, looking oh so effortlessly graceful and confident. Her posture is relaxed yet poised, showing she's got it all together.

When Kate stands tall, it makes everyone around her feel at ease. People feel more comfortable and confident because she comes across as stable and reliable; someone who is genuinely paying attention. Plus, her great posture shows she respects the event, setting a tone of importance, which subtly encourages everyone else to step up their game. And let's be honest, if a royal can pull off perfect posture without looking stiff, the rest of us have no excuse!

By maintaining good posture, we all can similarly exude confidence and demonstrate respect for the event or conversation.

The Place Setting

There are several types of place settings, each designed for a different type of meal or occasion and influenced by cultural or regional customs.

Here are the most common:

Basic, Casual, Buffet, Family Style, Formal

We're going to focus on the formal place setting because once you have learned this one, you can easily navigate the others.

As I stepped into the room, I was immediately captivated. The air felt different—warm yet crisp, like stepping into a world where every detail was curated

with care. The soft glow of candlelight danced off the polished silverware, casting delicate reflections that sparkled like diamonds. The room was majestic yet intimate, with rich velvet drapes that framed tall windows overlooking a sunset-soaked garden. Soft classical music filled the space, enhancing the atmosphere of timeless elegance.

But it was the table that left me speechless. A gleaming white linen tablecloth draped effortlessly over the grand dining table, its luxurious fabric grazing the floor. The china was nothing short of royal—a pristine bone-white with delicate gold trim, each plate a work of art. Crystal glassware sparkled in the light, their intricate cuts catching the glow from the chandelier above. Utensils—polished to perfection—were arranged symmetrically, from the smallest fork to the largest knife, each one seemingly waiting for its moment to shine. It felt as if every piece had a purpose, carefully laid out with respect and intention.

The centerpiece drew my eye next—a lush arrangement of fresh blooms. Roses, hydrangeas, and peonies in soft pinks, creams, and blushes stood tall in a crystal vase, their sweet fragrance wafting through the room. Ivy and delicate greenery trailed gracefully from the arrangement, bringing life to the refined atmosphere. The beauty of it all made me feel like royalty, cherished, and deeply welcomed into an experience far beyond dining—it was an invitation to an unforgettable moment, shared in exquisite company.

In that instant, I realized this wasn't just about food or drink; it was about connection, ceremony, and the celebration of fine living. Every element whispered, "You are important. You belong here."

Formal

1) Salad Fork 2) Dinner Fork 3) Dinner Knife 4) Teaspoon 5) Soup Spoon 6) Butter Knife 7) Dessert Fork 8) Dessert Spoon 9) Napkin 10) Salad Plate 11) Dinner Plate 12) Charger 13) Teacup 14) Saucer 15) Bread Plate 16) Water Glass 17) Wine Glass (white) 18) Champagne

Napkin can be placed on the table to the left of the Salad Fork

Missing:
Soup Bowl can be placed on top of the salad plate #10, if present
Red Wine Glass which is placed above the #17
Salad Knife to the right of the Dinner Knife #3
Oyster Fork to the right of the Soup Spoon #5
Fish Fork to the left of the Dinner Fork, if served first. In this instance, the Salad Fork would then be to the right of the Dinner Fork.

Note: Wherever you see "Dinner" you can replace it with "Entrée" because this includes lunch!

Informal

1) Dinner Fork 2) Dinner Knife 3) Spoon 4) Napkin 5) Dinner Plate 6) Charger is NOT included in this setting 7) Glass

<u>Note:</u> Napkin can be placed under the Dinner Fork #1
Wherever you see "Dinner" you can replace it with "Entrée" because this includes lunch!

Plate: The Centerpiece of Your Meal

First, there's a large plate called the dinner plate right in front of you. The main course, such as a succulent steak or exquisite pasta dish, will be presented here. It's right in the middle because it's the star of the show! Under the dinner plate, there may be a service plate or a charger. Chargers provide an elegant base for your dinnerware. Chargers come in a variety of colors and designs. We never eat off of the charger. It is used for decorative purposes or to protect a table from condensation or heat. Placemats can also be used instead of a charger. Placemats are practical and also decorative. They add a layer of texture and color to the table while protecting the tablecloth from spills.

On top of your dinner plate is your napkin.

Fork: The Elegant Essential

To the far left of the dinner plate, there's a shorter fork. This is called the salad fork. It's for eating salads or appetizers before the main course. It's smaller than the other fork because it doesn't need to do as much work.

To the right of the salad fork, there's another fork. This one is called the dinner fork. It's bigger and more robust for eating the main course. It is designed to handle heartier dishes with ease. You'll use this fork to dig into your delicious meal!

Notice that the FORK is on the LEFT side? Your salad and dinner forks should be to the left of your plate, with the dessert fork and spoon above it. Your knife and spoon are placed to the right of your plate. A great tip to remember is that F-O-R-K has four letters in it, like L-E-F-T, so your fork is placed on the left.

Your K-N-I-F-E and S-P-O-O-N have 5 letters in it like R-I-G-H-T, so they are placed on the right.

Knife: The Precision Tool

Now, we encounter a poised knife to the right of the dinner plate. This is your dinner knife, with the sharp edge facing the plate. Its purpose is clear – to cut, trim or slice through "all that goodness" awaiting your plate, whether it be a tender steak or savory poultry.

Next to the dinner knife, there's a smaller knife called the salad knife. It is used for cutting salads or other appetizers. It's smaller than the dinner knife because it doesn't need to cut through thick foods.

Moving on, your glass rests above the knife. One is a tall glass, called the water glass or goblet. This is where you'll find your water for sipping throughout the meal. Make sure to stay hydrated!

Beside the water goblet, there's another glass called the wine glass. Whether red, white, or rosé, it awaits to accentuate the meal's flavors with sophistication and refinement. In some settings, there may be a specific glass for red wine, white wine, or a flute for champagne. This is what they look like:

To the right of the knife, a spoon awaits. This is your soup spoon, a symbol of the refined dining experience. In some cases, a teacup and saucer, always pre-set, add a touch of elegance. They are located to the right of the spoon. Directly above the dinner plate, your dessert spoon and fork, if not present, will be provided when dessert is served. Notice the direction of the dessert fork and spoon. If they were cars, they would drive in the opposite direction, a subtle yet elegant detail.

Above the forks on the left, a small bread plate awaits. This is where you place your bread or roll, a small yet significant detail that shows your attention and consideration. You may be provided with a butter knife or a smaller regular knife. The blade should face downward, a sign of respect for the table setting and your fellow diners.

Napkin

As soon as you sit down, place the napkin in your lap. Do not snap or dramatically shake the napkin. Don't make a big production of unfolding your napkin. Discreetly unfold your napkin below the table and refold it with the crease towards you. Don't tuck your napkin into your shirt collar like a bib. If you are dining in someone's home, you should wait until the host or hostess places the napkin in their lap. This is a sign of respect for their role and helps them feel at ease. Use your napkin to dab your mouth as needed during the meal. Remember "Dapper Dan Always Dabs."

Use your napkin to blot any spills or stains on your clothing. Your napkin is not your washcloth. Don't use it to vigorously wipe your entire face, pat your sweat, or blow your nose. These cloth napkins are laundered, so please be considerate. If you need to speak with your server, please do not use your napkin to flag them down. Using a napkin to wave down the server is like a matador gracefully twirling their cape in the bullring, commanding attention. Beckon to them with two fingers (index and middle fingers together) in a gentle pulse or a closed wave.

Napkin rings can be an excellent addition to a formal setting. When you remove the napkin ring from your napkin, place it to the left of your plate.

Need to get up?

Don't crumple or fold your napkin into a ball. Place the napkin in your chair. Do not announce where you are going. For example, "I'll be right back; I'm going to the restroom." Say, "Excuse me!"

Once you finish dining, pinch your napkin in the center of the fold and place it loosely to the left of the dinner plate. Avoid placing your napkin on top of the dinner plate, which could lead to more stains on the napkin.

Remember that your napkin is intended to keep your clothing clean during the meal, so use it for that purpose only. This shows consideration. Avoid using it for anything that could be seen as unsanitary or impolite.

Bread

"How can a nation be great if its bread tastes like Kleenex?"
~Julia Child

(Oh, how we love our bread!) It could be the whole meal for some of us, but there's etiquette here, too!

If the bread basket is in front of you, you can pick it up and offer it to the person on your right.

Get excited because you do not need a knife or a fork! That's right, use your fingers. The key is to tear off bite-size pieces one at a time. Tear off a piece and then eat that piece before tearing off another piece. If you love to add butter to your bread, butter each piece at a time. If there is one butter dish for everyone to share, use your butter knife to remove a small pat of butter and place it on your bread and butter plate. You will then proceed to butter from your bread plate.

Avoid double fisting (holding your bread in your left hand while eating or drinking with your right hand). Remember which bread plate belongs to you, and if the glass in front of you belongs to you or your neighbor, use "b" and "d." Touch the index finger on your right hand to your right thumb. Touch the index finger on your left hand to your left thumb. The "b" formed by your left hand is for "bread" (your bread plate is always at the left of your place setting). The "d" formed by your right hand is for "drink" (your drinking glasses are always at the right of your place setting).

Utensils

Deciding which knife, fork, or spoon to use is made easier by the **outside-in rule**—use utensils on the outside first and work your way inward. So, if someone served a salad first, use the fork set to the far left of your plate.

Forks

Hold your fork like a pencil and not a pitchfork or gavel. First, balance the fork in your open hand (palm up) on your index finger. The handle should be laying inside the palm of your hand. Bend your last three fingers towards the center of your hand and turn your hand over, so that your index finger rests on the back of the fork.

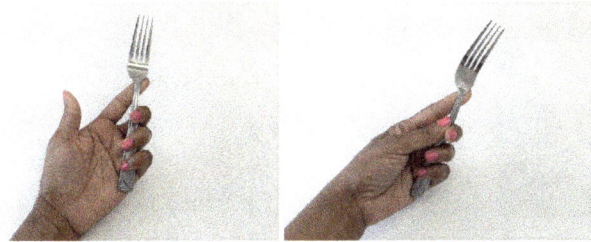

Knives

Do the same with your knife but in your right hand. Balance the knife in your open hand (palm up) on your index finger. The handle should be lying inside the palm of your hand. Bend the last three fingers towards the center of your hand and turn your hand over so that your index finger is now resting on the spine of the knife.

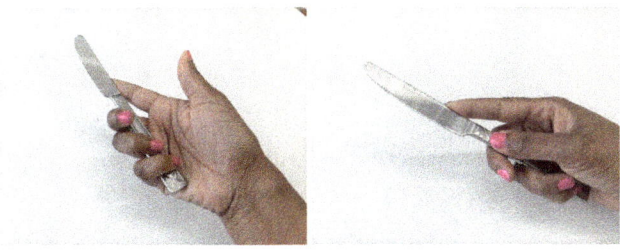

Glassware

Wine Glasses

When a meal is accompanied by wine, understanding the art of handling your wine glass is not just a skill, but a crucial element of the dining experience.

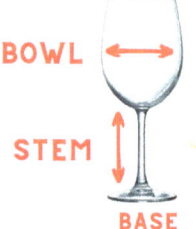

Hold the stem with your thumb and index finger while bracing your third finger and resting on the base. If you have a stemless glass, keep your fingers together and hold the bottom of the glass.

Avoid holding your glass by the bowl to avoid warming the wine with your hand, which could change the taste of your wine. For example, a crisp white wine is served chilled. Even though some reds are served at room temperature, we don't want to heat the wine to a body temp of 98.6.

A larger, rounder glass is used for red wine, while white wine glasses are typically narrower and tulip-shaped.

Champagne and Sparkling Wine Glasses

If you are celebrating with some bubbly, a fluted glass is the way to go. The tall, narrow design allows the bubbles to rise gracefully.

Dining Styles

American Style

There are various dining styles, but we will focus on American and Continental styles.

The American style, also known as the zig-zag method, is a less formal and straightforward style of dining widely practiced in the US and Canada. It is easy for anyone to adapt.

With both styles, place your knife in your dominant hand.

Firstly, balance the fork in your open hand (palm up) on your index finger. The handle should be lying inside the palm of your hand. Bend the last three fingers towards the center of your hand and turn your hand over so that your index finger rests on the back of the fork. Do the same with your knife but in your right hand.

Balance the knife in your open hand (palm up) on your index finger. The handle should be lying inside the palm of your hand. Bend the last three fingers towards the center of your hand and turn your hand over so that your index finger is now resting on the spine of the knife.

Pierce, the food with the fork, tines down. The knife cuts through the food, placing pressure on the handle with your index finger. Cut behind the fork and not in front or in between the tines. Avoid a "digging" action or aggressively sawing your food. The key is to cut a bite-size piece.

When cutting is done, the knife is balanced, and the blade is downward on the top edge of your plate. The fork is switched back into your right hand. Simultaneously, place your left hand in your lap. The food is placed in your mouth with the tines up.

After a few bites, take a break. Use your napkin to dab your mouth twice before taking a drink.

Place your utensils in the rest position to signal to the wait staff or your dining companions that you are taking a break. If you were looking at a clock, your fork would be positioned towards the left side of your plate with the tines up and the handle at 4:25 pm. The knife is balanced on the edge of your plate with the blade downward. You would also use the resting position when excusing yourself from the table.

Once you have finished dining, place your utensils in the finished position. If you were looking at a clock, it would look like 10:20 or 12:30.

Continental Style

Continental style is also known as European. This dining style is more formal and widely practiced in many parts of the world. Continental-style dining is typically used in formal dining settings, such as upscale restaurants, fine dining events, and formal dinners, where adherence to traditional etiquette is valued. In this dining style, the fork is held in the left hand and the knife in the right hand throughout the meal, without switching hands like in American dining. Once you cut your food, rest your wrist on the edge of the table and lift your left hand to your mouth with the tines of the fork pointing downward. Avoid leaning down into your food or waving your utensils like an orchestra conductor.

Place your utensils in the rest position to signal to the wait staff or your dining companions that you are taking a break. If you were looking at a clock in this position, the knife is resting on your plate with the handle hanging off of the plate at 10:20. Remember, the blade is downward. The fork is inverted, with the tines downward and the tips of the knife and fork meeting each other. It is also acceptable to place the inverted tines over the knife.

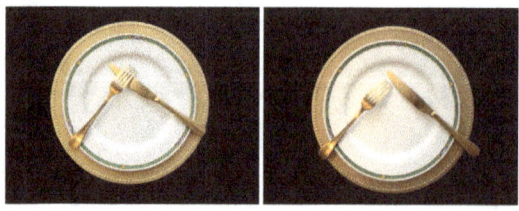

This dining style is often considered more efficient and elegant, as it reduces the need for frequent hand-switching and enables a smoother dining experience.

Informal Dining
Good Vibes, Good Manners

I nformal or casual dining scenarios are more relaxed but still require manners and respect. Here are some ways to approach them:

Observation

As soon as you arrive at an event, observe the place settings, the atmosphere, and the attire of the other diners. These visual cues will provide insights into the formality of the event.

Follow the Host

In both formal and informal settings, the host or hostess plays a crucial role in guiding the tone of the meal. Their actions and choices should be your benchmark, as they set the standard for your behavior and choices throughout the meal.

Comfortable Posture

Maintain good posture to show respect and attentiveness.

Attire Matters

Your attire should always align with the formality of the event. While overdressing can be awkward, underdressing can be disrespectful.

Serving Etiquette

In informal settings, food may be served family-style or buffet-style. For family-style dining, wait until the host starts serving or invites guests to begin. When passing dishes, always pass to the right and avoid reaching across the table. If it's a buffet, be considerate not to pile your plate high, leaving enough for other guests. Can I go back for seconds? Yes, you can! Just glance around to be sure that everyone has been served.

Timing and Pace

Even in a relaxed setting, try to pace your eating to match the other guests. Rushing through your meal can come across as impatient, while lingering too long may delay the next course or the clearing of plates. Paying attention to others' pace helps create a comfortable dining rhythm and won't leave you looking around at the others.

Handling Shared Dishes and Condiments

Casual dining may involve sharing condiments, sauces, or dips. Avoid directly dipping your food into shared bowls; instead, use the serving utensils to scoop a small amount onto your plate or pour onto your plate. This keeps things clean. Additionally, if a guest needs something like salt or pepper, pass both shakers together (they're married) to avoid breaking the traditional etiquette rule.

Casual Table Manners

Informal dining doesn't eliminate the need for good table manners. Chew with your mouth closed, avoid talking with food in your mouth, and don't use your phone at the table unless it's essential. Casual environments may feel more forgiving, but adhering to these basics shows respect and mindfulness.

Responding to Unexpected Situations

Unexpected situations can arise—a dropped fork, spilled drink, or a minor mishap. Remain calm, acknowledge it gracefully, and if necessary, ask the host discreetly for assistance.

Simplified Place Settings

Informal dining usually includes fewer utensils. Start with your outermost utensils and work inward. If you need more clarification, follow the lead of your host or hostess.

Napkin Use

The process of using your napkin remains the same, whether dining formally or informally. Unfold it and place it on your lap when seated, use it as needed during the meal, and leave it to the left of your plate when finished. Remember to dab, dab, dab!

Relaxed Conversation

In this setting, it allows for a broader range of conversation topics. However, always be mindful of others' comfort and avoid controversial subjects.

Beverage Choices

Informal dining may include a variety of beverage choices, including non-alcoholic options. Be aware of the etiquette for ordering and consuming beverages.

Thanking the Host

After the meal, expressing gratitude to the host is a thoughtful touch that leaves a positive impression. A simple, sincere "Thank you for hosting" goes a long way, and if the gathering was particularly enjoyable, consider following up with a short message or thank you note later. This courtesy acknowledges the host's effort and shows your appreciation for their hospitality.

Au Revoir

When it's time to leave, thank the host once again and say goodbye to other guests. Avoid leaving too abruptly, as this can feel dismissive; instead, take a moment to express that you enjoyed the evening. If there is an established end time, be mindful not to linger too long afterward unless the host encourages you to stay. Don't overstay your welcome.

Sip and Savor

Mr. Grateful

As the evening unfolded at a lavish gala, where I was serving as the etiquette consultant, I found myself surrounded by dazzling lights, elegant attire, and a sea of sophisticated, high-profile individuals. My task for the evening was to ensure that every guest felt comfortable and confident in their manners—a role I took immense satisfaction with.

Among the crowd was a delightful gentleman whom I'll call "Mr. Graceful." Despite his charm and refinement, he found himself confronted with a classic dining dilemma: the wine list. When he opened it, his expression revealed a mix of awe and uncertainty as he skimmed over an intimidating array of French and Italian names.

It reminded me of my early days, facing wine menus with the same wide-eyed trepidation, not knowing a Cabernet from a Merlot. I chuckled, recalling my own journey of learning—thanks to friends who were sommeliers and a few well-attended wine tastings where I learned to navigate the basics.

With that memory fresh, I approached Mr. Graceful with a warm smile and shared how I, too, had once felt bewildered by wine lists. He laughed, admitting he only knew he wanted "something red." Together, we took a lighthearted approach to deciphering the list, sampling flavors, and exploring new varieties. Our shared learning moment was a beautiful reminder that the world of fine dining, as refined as it is, always holds room for discovery and laughter.

Here are a few wine tips to get you started:

Reading the Wine List

When faced with an extensive wine list, don't be overwhelmed. Start by looking at the wine's origin, type, and vintage. If you're unfamiliar with a particular wine, don't hesitate to ask your server for recommendations.

Pairing Wine with Food

Wine pairing can enhance your dining experience. Light wines like Pinot Grigio complement seafood, while bold reds like Cabernet Sauvignon pair well with red meats. Ask for recommendations from your server if you're uncertain.

Deciphering the Wine Label

Wine labels can appear complex, but they hold essential information. Learn to read labels to understand the grape variety, region, and vintage. The year on the label represents the harvest year of the grapes.

Wine Service

When the wine is served, examine the label to ensure it's the one you ordered. The server will pour a small amount into your glass for you to taste. Swirl it gently, sniff, and sip to confirm its quality. If it's satisfactory, nod to indicate your approval.

Sip and Savor

When savoring spirits, take your time. Sip it slowly to appreciate its flavors and aromas. Don't rush through the experience; savor every moment.

Cocktail Pairing

If you're having a cocktail with your meal, consider how its flavors complement your food. For example, a fruity cocktail might pair well with spicy cuisine, while a classic cocktail can enhance a steak dinner. Ask for recommendations from your server if you're uncertain.

Hosting with Grace

If you're hosting a dinner, be sure to have a variety of wines and spirits on hand to accommodate your guests' preferences. Offering a range of choices shows thoughtfulness and hospitality.

Responsible Consumption

Enjoying wine and spirits is a pleasurable part of the dining experience, but it's crucial to do so responsibly. Know your limits and never drink and drive.

The world of wine and spirits is a rich and fascinating one, offering endless opportunities for exploration and enjoyment. By understanding the fundamentals of wine selection, service, and appreciation, as well as mastering the etiquettes of handling wine and spirits, you'll not only enhance your dining experience but also showcase your sophistication. If you're passionate about wine and spirits, consider educating yourself further. Attend tastings, visit vineyards or get a sommelier bestie like I did, and deepen your knowledge.

My friend Nikia, WSET Level 3 Wines Certified

Too Much Drink, or You May Shrink!

Irresponsible Consumption

It's important to note that holiday work parties, conferences, company picnics are still an extension of your work or employment. Save the partying for another time, on your dime! If you're going to drink, I suggest a limit of 1-2 drinks.

Drinking too much at a holiday work party or conference can have various negative consequences, including:

Impaired Judgment

Excessive alcohol consumption can impair your judgment, leading to poor decision-making and inappropriate behavior. This could result in saying or doing things you might regret later.

Professional Reputation

Behaving inappropriately due to excessive drinking can damage your professional reputation. Colleagues and managers may perceive you as unreliable, unprofessional, or lacking self-control.

Career Consequences

Engaging in inappropriate behavior at a work-related event due to overdrinking can have serious career consequences, such as reprimands, demotions, or even termination, particularly if it violates company policies or codes of conduct.

Relationship Strain

Drinking excessively at a work function may strain relationships with colleagues, supervisors, or clients. It can create tension or discomfort in professional interactions and diminish trust and respect.

Legal Issues

If your behavior escalates to the point of breaking the law, such as driving under the influence or causing public disturbances, you may face legal consequences, including fines, license suspension, or even incarceration.

Embarrassment

Excessive drinking can lead to embarrassing situations, such as slurred speech, stumbling, or vomiting in public, which can be humiliating and difficult to recover from professionally.

Missed Opportunities

Being intoxicated at a work event may cause you to miss valuable networking opportunities or fail to make a positive impression on key individuals who could further your career.

Loss of Respect

Colleagues and supervisors may lose respect for you if they witness or hear about your excessive drinking behavior, which can damage relationships and hinder your professional growth.

I know that's a lot to think about but the investment in your education and career is worth it! So have a good time but use your discretion!

Toasting Etiquette

When toasting, raise your glass and make eye contact with the person you're toasting. Offer a brief, heartfelt sentiment, and clink glasses gently. Never clink the rim of the glass, as this could cause it to break.

If you are presenting a toast, you may sit or stand, as long as you can be seen and heard. Toasts are usually presented by the host at the beginning of the meal, while others can present their toasts during dessert. With so much excitement in the air it can be a bit challenging trying to get everyone's attention. Avoid banging on the table, or any other loud interruptions. You can use a chime or bell or a microphone.

Before you begin your toast, look around to ensure everyone's glass is filled including the non-alcoholic drinkers.

Here are the 3s of a toast:

Your toast should be **S**uccinct (short), **S**ituational (in line with the occasion) and **S**incere.

Replying to a Toast

When toasted, the "toastee" does not stand, unless you've been asked to rise. Nor does she drink to herself.

Once the toast is finished, the toastee simply acknowledges the toast with a "thank you." She may then stand and raise her own glass to propose a toast to the host or anyone else she wants to honor.

A TOAST TO YOU

Let's raise our glasses to each and every one of you fabulous folks. Seriously, you're all rockstars for joining us on this journey of culinary refinement. Your dedication to upping your dining game is seriously inspiring. Cheers to you for taking the plunge and diving into the world of impeccable table manners with us. Let's not just devour our food, but also soak in the wisdom and laughs that come with it. Because let's face it, who knew that holding a fork a certain way could be so entertaining?

Cheers to you all, and may your dining experiences always be a reflection of the elegance and grace that define you!

Bon appétit!

Soup Etiquette – Some like it HOT

U sually soup is served hot unless you're having soupe froide or Gazpacho. You have now been served after eagerly awaiting the soup course. "Ugh, it's too hot!" Whatever you do, do not blow on your hot soup. Wait for it to cool down or stir in the shape of a half-moon crescent at the top of your soup plate.

Dip the spoon sideways into the soup at the near edge of the bowl, then skim from the front of the bowl to the back. Sip from the side of the spoon but no slurping is allowed.

To retrieve the last spoonful of soup, slightly tip the bowl away from you and spoon in the way that works best. It's been said that the only 2 countries that you can dunk or sop up your soup with bread are France and Italy. When you're finished, leave your spoon in your soup dish. If you were served a soup cup, place your spoon on the saucer or underplate.

In dining etiquette, "double fisting" refers to the somewhat casual act of holding two items in each hand simultaneously—like a bowl or cup of soup in one hand and a slice of bread or roll in the other. For some of us that's called "good eatin' !" While it may be tempting, especially on a cold day, to cradle your soup bowl in one hand while nibbling on a piece of bread in the other, this approach veers away from traditional dining decorum.

When it comes to soup etiquette, it's best to give each item its due time and attention, allowing for a more polished dining experience. Instead of double-fisting, you could enjoy the soup first. Once you've finished or set down the spoon, then take a small bite of bread, ideally breaking off only one bite-sized piece at a time. This creates a balanced and elegant rhythm to the meal, letting you savor the flavors without looking rushed or overly casual.

While double-fisting may feel practical, especially in more relaxed settings, taking the time to alternate between spooning your soup and enjoying the bread with intention aligns better with dining etiquette and brings a greater sense of sophistication to the table.

In the upcoming chapter, we'll delve deeper into the intricacies of dining etiquette, including mastering dining gestures and conversations and handling the challenges that can arise during dining. So, let's continue this journey to dining excellence together.

Mastering Dining Gestures and Conversations

I n my early days as an etiquette consultant, I found myself dining at one of Atlanta's finest establishments, with a client named Markus. We were celebrating his recent promotion, and he had invited me to dinner to brush up on his dining etiquette in preparation for an upcoming business trip. As we sat at the beautifully set table, I couldn't help but smile—this was one of those moments where my passion for etiquette truly intersected with real life.

Now, Markus was a brilliant professional, but when it came to fine dining, he was more "let's keep it casual" than "polished perfection." As we perused the menu, he began enthusiastically recounting his recent skiing trip. And when I say "enthusiastically," I mean full sound effects and grand gestures—he practically recreated his downhill slope with his fork in hand!

I sat there, politely amused. I could see the eyes of the other diners subtly turning toward us. While I appreciated Markus's energy and the joy he found in his story, I knew this was a teachable moment.

After his animated reenactment, I gently smiled and said, "Markus, I love your enthusiasm. It's clear that you had a fantastic time. But in settings like this, we dial back the big gestures. We want to match the elegance of the environment and keep our conversations more refined—kind of like the smooth ride up the ski lift before the downhill adventure!"

Markus chuckled, realizing he had gotten a bit carried away. He relaxed into a quieter, more poised version of himself for the rest of the evening. We shared laughter, insightful conversation, and by the end of the night, Markus had not only picked up a few etiquette tips but also understood how subtle gestures and polished conversation can enhance the dining experience for everyone at the table.

In that moment, I saw firsthand how important it is to balance the places and people we share special moments with—especially at the dinner table. Dining is not just about the food; it's about creating an experience that's enjoyable for everyone. And that, my friends, is how you dine and shine.

Dining Posture and Non-verbal Communication

Your dining posture and non-verbal communication say a lot about you. Maintaining the right posture and demeanor is essential to projecting confidence and respect at the table. Here's how to ensure you make the right impression:

Sitting Up Straight

Just as in the previous chapters, maintaining good posture is crucial. Sit up straight, but not rigid. Keep your back comfortably against the chair, with your shoulders relaxed.

Elegance in Motion

When using utensils, aim for smooth and controlled movements. Avoid clanging utensils or making loud, abrupt sounds. Your movements should be fluid and unobtrusive. Remember you're not a matador, at least not here!

Non-verbal Listening

When someone is speaking, maintain eye contact to show that you're actively listening and engaged in the conversation. Avoid appearing distracted or disinterested even though you've been waiting all afternoon to eat the Branzino.

Darting eyes send a message that you're killing time and that you are not really interested. Conversely, don't hold people hostage. You can usually tell or feel when they are ready to move on. You know, they're looking around, give you one-word responses, glance down at their watch—LET THEM GO!

Control Gestures

While excitement and enthusiasm are great, over-exuberant gestures can disrupt the dining experience. Be mindful of the space and comfort of those around you.

Maintain Composure

If something unexpected occurs during the meal, like spilling a drink or food, maintain your composure and address the situation calmly. Remember, accidents happen to the best of us.

Engaging in Polite Dinner Conversations

Dinner conversations are a vital part of the dining experience. Engaging in polite and meaningful conversations not only enhances your dining experience but also makes you a charming and enjoyable dining companion. Here are some tips for mastering the art of dinner conversations:

Topics

Begin with pleasant greetings and light topics. Keep it light and positive. Avoid sensitive or controversial subjects like politics or personal problems. Instead, discuss travel, hobbies, entertainment, or shared interests. While enjoying a delicious dinner at one of my favorite restaurants in Richmond, Virginia, my guests and I were shocked by the conversation at the next table. These folks were speaking so loudly, we couldn't help to hear one of the ladies at that table talk about her gastric surgery and recovery. YESSS...at the table!!! Believe me, we were not ear hustling as they say in the south but it was unavoidable. This is a NO NO! What you say and do at your table is your business but I kindly ask that you maintain a low volume to spare the rest of us!

Active Listening

Show genuine interest in what others are saying. Ask open-ended questions and actively listen to their responses. This encourages a two-way flow of conversation. Conversations are like a tennis match. Keep that ball going back and forth!

Be Inclusive

Pay attention to all the diners at the table. Engage with those around you, making sure no one feels left out or excluded from the conversation.

Respect Opinions

Everyone has different opinions and perspectives. Even if you disagree with someone, maintain respect for their point of view and avoid confrontations or arguments.

Table Manners During Conversations

During conversations, be mindful of your table manners. Avoid speaking with your mouth full, interrupting others, or shouting across the table. Wait for an appropriate moment to speak.

Managing Difficult Topics

If a sensitive or difficult topic arises, navigate it with grace. Offer your perspective without dominating the conversation or making others uncomfortable. Use diplomacy and if possible steer the conversation toward a more neutral subject.

Silence is Okay

Don't feel compelled to fill every moment with conversation. Comfortable silences are a part of any good dining experience. Allow moments for everyone to savor their food and enjoy the ambiance.

Dealing with Difficult Dining Scenarios

You may occasionally encounter challenging situations that test your poise and etiquette. Here are some common dining scenarios and tips on how to handle them gracefully:

Dining with Picky Eaters

If you're dining with someone who has specific dietary preferences or restrictions, choose a restaurant that accommodates their needs. Be understanding and non-judgmental about their choices.

Dealing with Rude Guests

If you're unfortunate enough to dine with a rude or difficult guest, your best approach is to remain polite and composed. Avoid confrontation and focus on enjoying the company of those who are pleasant and polite. If your dining companion continues to be rude or you feel embarrassed, it may be a good idea to end your dinner early by politely and gracefully excusing yourself. Hmmm, perhaps a little white lie?

- "I'm not feeling very well suddenly. I think I might need to head home and rest."

- "I just received an important phone call that I need to take care of immediately."

- Or you can sincerely ask them a question (try to not sound judgy)"Are you feeling ok?" "Would you rather go somewhere else or go out another evening when you can enjoy this much better?"

Food Mishaps

Spills, falls, and food mishaps can happen to anyone. If you're the one affected, calmly address the situation, and if you're a bystander, show empathy and offer assistance if needed. Typically when a utensil or food item falls to the ground; you would alert the wait staff so they can replace the utensil or attend to the mess. I know you are considerate and want to showcase your best table manners but where would you place the soiled item? On a plate or on the tablecloth? As you can see, you could not place it comfortably back on the table so allow the wait staff to continue to serve.

Removing Unwanted Food from your Mouth

Food is removed from the mouth in the manner in which it is put into the mouth. I can see that puzzled look on your face. This one is a little more difficult to digest. Food put into the mouth with a utensil is removed with a utensil. When fingers are used to eat food, the pit or bone is removed with fingers.

Unpleasant Food

If you're served food that doesn't meet your expectations, avoid making a scene. Simply let your server know politely and discreetly. They will usually address the issue and find a suitable solution.

Dining Etiquette Blunders

If you witness a fellow diner making a dining etiquette mistake, it's best to discreetly overlook it. Correcting someone at the table can be embarrassing for them.

Dealing with Tricky Foods

Twirl Spaghetti like a Star

Whether it is spaghetti or some other pasta, there is an etiquette as well. There is still an age-old debate as to whether you should use a spoon to assist your swirling method. Generally, formal etiquette consists of using your fork only. Insert your fork into your plate near the edge, this helps in balancing the tines of the fork and then wound up a few strands. Twirl until you have a neat little bundle of spaghetti on your fork. If a strand of spaghetti dangles, don't suck it in. Instead, use the edge of your fork or a small piece of bread to guide it into your mouth.

If you choose to eat with a spoon which is considered a faux pas to some or acceptable to others in a casual setting, this is what you do.

Imagine your fork and spoon are dance partners. The spoon holds the spaghetti while the fork twirls it around. This keeps things tidy and elegant. Use the spoon to help steady the fork if you need to. Twirl until you have a neat little bundle of spaghetti on your fork. If a strand of spaghetti dangles, don't suck it in. Instead, use the edge of your fork or a small piece of bread to guide it into your mouth.

Corn on the cob

Eating corn on the cob can be both fun and a little tricky to do elegantly. Here are a few tips to enjoying this summer favorite with good manners.

1. Your corn on the cob is a canvas, and you're an artist. Use a small butter knife to spread butter evenly across the corn.

2. If you like salt or other seasonings, sprinkle them gently while holding the corn over your plate to catch any excess.

3. You can use your fingers to hold the ends firmly or if you prefer less mess, use those cute little corn holders.

4. Now imagine that you're typing out a letter on an old-fashioned type-writer. Start at one end of the corn and take neat, small bites in a row across the cob. Bite down firmly but not too deeply to avoid getting kernels stuck in your teeth. Once you finish a row, rotate the cob and start a new row.

5. Are you ready for this one? Keep your napkin close because you'll need it. If butter gets on your fingers, resist the temptation to lick them. Keep it in your lap and use it frequently to dab your mouth and fingers.

Pizza, Pizza!!□

Yes, pizza etiquette exists! While pizza is often associated with casual dining, there are still a few key guidelines to keep in mind, especially in certain settings. Can you eat with your hands or should you use utensils?

In a casual setting, it's perfectly acceptable to eat pizza with your hands, especially at pizzerias or informal gatherings.

If you're at a more formal dining event or in certain cultures (like in Italy), you may be expected to use a knife and fork, especially with thin-crust pizza or when the pizza is served uncut. In this case start cutting from the tip to the crust.

Serving Others

If you're sharing a pizza with a group, it's polite to let everyone serve themselves, ensuring each person gets an equal amount of slices. Avoid taking the biggest or the last slice without offering it to others first.

Fold or No Fold

In places like New York, folding your slice lengthwise is common and considered normal. However, in other regions, eating pizza flat is the standard. If you prefer a Chicago style pizza, which is deep dish style with thicker crust, a knife and fork could come in handy and make it less messy. There's no right or wrong way, but if you're traveling, it's good to observe local customs. When in Rome...

Pizza can range from a casual meal to part of an elegant dining experience, so adjusting your approach to fit the setting is key!

"I Would Like to buy a Hamburger"

Did you guess the scene? It's Steve Martin in *The Pink Panther* (2006) trying to say, "I would like to buy a hamburger!"' in that unforgettable French accent—grace is key, even if the pronunciation isn't!

Picture this, a perfectly cooked beef patty, juicy and full of flavor, grilled to a succulent medium. It's topped with crisp lettuce, vine-ripened tomato slices, a dollop of creamy mayo, a squirt of ketchup, and a few slivers of fresh onions. The warm, slightly toasted bun has just the right amount of softness to hold everything together without falling apart. Add to that a slice of melted cheddar cheese and perhaps a couple of tangy pickles for that extra zing, and you've got a burger that's hard to resist.

Now, you might be thinking: can something as simple as eating a hamburger have etiquette? Well, it kinda does, but don't worry—it's pretty straightforward, and you can still savor every bite!

1. Cutting It Down to Size
   If your burger is stacked high or a bit on the larger side, it's perfectly acceptable—even smart—to cut it in half or quarters. This makes it easier to handle and prevents everything from spilling out on the first bite. Once it's more manageable, feel free to use your fingers to pick up each piece and enjoy.

2. Proper Hand Position
   If you're tackling the whole burger without cutting it, there's a handy technique to keep everything intact. Use your thumb and pinkie to hold the bottom of the burger while your remaining three fingers rest on top, gently pressing down to keep the fillings secure. This grip not only provides support but also ensures that you don't lose any toppings mid-bite.

3. Flipping the Burger
   Believe it or not, some people swear by flipping their burger upside down before taking a bite. The theory is that the thicker top bun absorbs more of the juices, preventing the bottom bun from getting soggy. Try it out—it might just change your burger game!

4. Eating in Bites, Not Gulps
   While it can be tempting to take a massive bite out of your burger, it's

more polite to take smaller, manageable bites. Not only does this prevent any awkward "stuffed mouth" moments, but it also ensures you savor the flavors and textures in each bite.

5. Use a Napkin or Two!!
Burgers can get messy, especially when they're loaded with sauces and toppings. Always have a napkin handy, and don't be shy about using it. Wipe your hands and mouth regularly to stay tidy, especially if you're in a social setting.

6. Condiments and Customization
If you're dining with others, avoid making a mess with condiments. If you need to add more ketchup, mustard, or other sauces, do it carefully, without overloading and risking a spill.

7. Be Considerate
Some toppings, like onions or pickles, can have strong flavors. Be mindful of your breath when eating in close company and make sure to freshen up if needed!

Hamburger etiquette is really just about making sure you enjoy your meal while being mindful of those around you. So, go ahead—savor that delicious, juicy burger, and eat it with confidence!

Asparagus

Depending on how the asparagus is served, firm or soft will determine if you can use your fingers. If it is unsauced and firm, you can use your fingers but if it is softer and drizzled with a sauce, use your fork and knife.

Cherry Tomatoes

Ah, cherry tomatoes—so cute, so innocent, and yet so likely to launch themselves across the room like tiny tomato torpedoes. I love them, but when they sneak into my salad, even I cringe a little. But hey, we're not going to let these little guys win, right? They think they're tricky, but we've got moves.

Stealth Mode: Activated

When you spot one of these slippery little tomatoes on your plate, don't panic. You've got options! First, go into stealth mode: carefully spear that cherry tomato with your fork to steady it. Then, with the precision of a seasoned ninja, gently slice it in half with your knife. Yes, this does take some practice. And yes, you may have a few tomato casualties along the way, but hey, no one becomes a cherry tomato master overnight.

If All Else Fails...

If slicing it doesn't work (and trust me, there will be days when the tomato just isn't cooperating), it's perfectly fine to throw in the towel and leave it on your plate. Not every battle is worth fighting, especially when the alternative is getting splattered with tomato juice mid-conversation.

The Finger-Pop Method

Now, if you're dealing with cherry tomatoes outside the realm of salad—say, in a veggie tray or on the side—feel free to ditch the cutlery. Pop that little guy straight into your mouth with your fingers. It's quick, easy, and you'll avoid any potential salad shrapnel flying across the table.

Bonus Tip: The Squeeze Test

Before attempting to cut one, give your cherry tomato a gentle squeeze with the fork. If it feels like it's going to explode like a water balloon, just leave it whole and eat it in one bite. Trust me, nobody wants a tomato juice fountain.

So there you have it—how to survive the cherry tomato challenge with humor and grace. We're not letting these tiny troublemakers win!

Salad

Salad may seem like a harmless dish—just some leafy greens and veggies, right? But don't be fooled! Salad has its own set of etiquette rules, and knowing them can keep you from looking like a rookie at the dinner table. Let's dive into the world of salad with some etiquette tips to help you crunch with class.

Just a note that in Canada and the U.S., we tend to serve our salad before the main course whereas in other countries, the salad is served after the main course. Some may consider it an aid to digestion. The fiber in the greens and vegetables helps to "cleanse the palate" and move food through the digestive system. It's like hitting the reset button after a rich, savory meal.

After enjoying flavorful or heavy dishes, a salad with its crisp, cool ingredients can cleanse the palate, preparing you for dessert. The acidity from vinegar-based dressings in particular can help cut through the richness of the main course, leaving your mouth feeling refreshed.

Before you dig into your salad, check to see if your salad is chopped up in smaller bite size pieces. If it is, you won't need to pick up your knife, if it has been set. In most formal settings, salad is a *fork-only* affair. You're usually expected to tackle it with just your fork. If your salad is served with a protein, please use your fork and knife. Do not cut up your entire salad at one time. Remember to cut bite size pieces. Pace yourself and chew thoroughly.

Let's talk lettuce!

There's always that one piece of lettuce that's bigger than your face, flopping around your plate like it owns the place. Instead of stuffing the whole leaf in your mouth or cutting it with your knife, the etiquette is to fold it with your fork into a bite-sized portion. Gently tuck the edges in like you're folding a towel. This way you don't feel like you're wrestling with your greens.

The Dressing

Have you heard that less is more? When it comes to dressing, less is more. Don't drown your salad in a gallon of ranch, or you'll risk turning your plate into a soggy mess. In formal settings, if you're given the option, pour dressing sparingly, and if someone else is dressing it for you, don't hesitate to say "just a little, please." Better to err on the side of too little than too much—you can always add more, but you can't take it off once it's on there!

Pay attention here because this has happened to all of us! Ever had that moment where a rogue crouton or slice of cucumber makes a break for it? If something goes rogue and rolls off your plate, the best thing to do is leave it there. No need to chase it down the table—it's already a lost cause. I know you're gasping, don't make a to-do about it. Just smile and keep going like it never happened.

Spinach and other leafy greens have a sneaky way of getting stuck in your teeth. After a few bites, subtly check your teeth (a quick swipe with your tongue works) to make sure you're not carrying around a leafy souvenir for the rest of the meal. It's tempting but don't use your knife as a mirror or worse pull out your dental floss. If you feel that leafy souvenir, excuse yourself to remove it.

So, the next time you're facing a plate of greens, fear not! With these salad etiquette tips in your pocket, you can munch with elegance and avoid any leafy misadventures.

Seafood

Fish Etiquette: How to Eat Fish with Elegance

Eating fish can be elegant, whether you're enjoying filets or a whole fish. Here's a simple guide to doing it with style:

1. Tools

   - *Fish Knife & Fork*
     Use the knife to gently separate the meat, not to cut.

   - *Lemon & Sauces*
     Add sparingly to avoid overpowering the fish.

2. Eating Filets

   - *Gentle Flaking*
     Lightly break off bite-sized pieces. No sawing needed.

   - *Removing Skin*
     If you don't want the skin, use the knife to peel it off neatly.

3. Whole Fish

- *Top Fillet First*
  Cut along the backbone and remove in pieces. Lift the spine before eating the bottom fillet and remove bones discreetly by placing them on your plate.

4. Dealing with Bones

- If you have already started eating, use your tongue to move the bone to the front, then discreetly remove it with your hand and place it aside.

5. Formal Settings

- *Take Your Time*
  Wait for everyone to be served and pace yourself.

- Use your napkin to dab gently to stay clean, as fish can be oily.

6. Finger Bowls

- If provided, use them to clean your hands discreetly.

By following these steps, you'll enjoy your fish meal with ease and elegance!

Lobster Etiquette: How to Enjoy Lobster with Grace

Lobster can be a delicious, luxurious dish, but it's also one of those meals that can make even the most elegant diners feel a little clumsy. Here's a guide to handling lobster with finesse, whether you're at a fancy restaurant or hosting a seafood feast.

1. Handling Lobster Tools

- *Lobster Cracker*
  Use this to break open the claws and legs. Grip the claw in one hand and gently apply pressure with the cracker to avoid splattering.

- *Lobster Fork*
  This small, slender fork is for extracting meat from the shell. Use it to gently pull meat from hard-to-reach places like the claws or knuckles.

- ○ *Seafood Pick*
  A pick can help you access smaller pieces of meat inside the shell.

- ○ *Napkins or a Bib*
  Many restaurants offer bibs when serving lobster, and while it may not seem glamorous, using one is perfectly acceptable! If you're hosting, consider offering wet wipes for a quick cleanup.

2. Dissecting the Lobster

- ○ *Start with the Claws*
  Twist off the claws and crack them open with the lobster cracker. Be careful to avoid making a mess, and use the fork to remove the meat.

- ○ *Move to the Tail*
  Turn the lobster on its back, hold the tail, and bend it backward until it breaks free. Use your hands or fork to pull the meat out in one piece. Be mindful to remove the dark vein running through the tail (it's the digestive tract and not meant to be eaten).

- ○ *Legs & Knuckles*
  For the legs, twist and pull them off. Suck the meat out or use a pick to extract the meat. Knuckles can be tricky, so use the cracker to get them open.

3. Dipping in Butter

- ○ *Butter Etiquette*
  When dipping lobster meat in butter, use a fork or your fingers, depending on the setting. Always dip delicately—no need to submerge the meat as if it's on a rescue mission!

- ○ *Avoid Dripping*
  After dipping, pause for a moment to let the excess butter drip off, preventing splatters on your plate or clothes.

4. Conversation Etiquette

- *Timing*
  Lobster requires some focus at least for me, so if you're talking, try to pause before you start cracking and dissecting. It's easier to engage in conversation after you've gathered a manageable bite on your fork!

- *Polite Dining*
  Be mindful not to be too noisy with cracking and sucking, even though some sounds are inevitable. Eating slowly and neatly is key despite the wild popularity of ASMR videos!

5. Cleanup Etiquette

- *Finger Bowls*
  Some restaurants provide a finger bowl with warm water and lemon to clean your hands. Use it discreetly, dipping your fingers lightly and drying them with a napkin. Other restaurants offer wet wipes.

- *Napkin Usage*
  Keep your napkin on your lap during the meal and use it frequently to wipe your hands and mouth to avoid any butter smudges.

6. Special Considerations

- *Shell Disposal*
  Place shells on the designated side plate or dish. If there isn't one, discreetly set them to the side of your main plate.

- *Finishing*
  After finishing, make sure to wipe your hands thoroughly, and if you're at a restaurant, fold your bib neatly and place it on the table.

Enjoying lobster is all about balancing indulgence with grace. With these etiquette tips, you'll be able to navigate a lobster meal with style and confidence, leaving a lasting impression—without leaving butter stains!

DINING ETIQUETTE SIMPLIFIED

Oyster Etiquette: How to Enjoy Cooked and Raw Oysters with Style

Whether you're slurping down raw oysters or savoring a plate of cooked oysters, dining on these shellfish requires a bit of finesse. Here's your guide to navigating both cooked and raw oysters with confidence and grace.

1. Raw Oysters
   The Basics - The Right Tools

   ○ *Oyster Fork*
     A small, three-pronged fork is typically provided to loosen the oyster from its shell.

   ○ *Lemon Wedges & Sauces*
     Fresh lemon, mignonette (vinegar-based sauce), cocktail sauce, and hot sauce are commonly served with raw oysters.

2. Preparing to Eat Raw Oysters

   ○ *Check the Oyster*
     Always check for freshness. The oyster should smell like the ocean—if it has a strong, fishy odor, it may be bad. If in doubt, ask the server.

   ○ *Loosen the Oyster*
     Gently use the oyster fork to ensure the oyster is detached from the shell, as it can sometimes stick.

   ○ *Hold the Shell Properly*
     Grip the oyster by the wider, deeper part of the shell to avoid spilling the "liquor" (the briny liquid).

3. Eating Raw Oysters

   ○ *To Slurp or Not to Slurp*
     It's perfectly acceptable to slurp raw oysters directly from the shell. Tilt the shell towards your mouth and let the oyster and liquor slide in.

- ○ *Chew vs. Swallow*
  Some people swallow oysters whole, but for the full experience, give it a gentle chew or two to release the flavors.

- ○ *Adding Condiments*
  A light squeeze of lemon or a small spoonful of mignonette adds a tangy kick. If you prefer cocktail or hot sauce, use them sparingly to avoid overpowering the oyster's natural brininess.

4. Cooked Oysters
The Basics – Cooked oysters can be prepared in a variety of ways, including grilled, fried, or baked. These are often richer in flavor and offer a different texture than raw oysters.

Common Dishes:

- ○ Oysters Rockefeller: Baked with breadcrumbs, butter, and spinach.

- ○ Grilled Oysters: Often served with garlic butter or Parmesan cheese.

- ○ Fried Oysters: Lightly breaded and fried, often served with a dipping sauce.

5. Eating Cooked Oysters

- ○ *No Need to Slurp*
  Cooked oysters are generally eaten with a fork. Use the oyster fork to scoop out the oyster meat rather than slurping it from the shell.

- ○ *Cut Larger Oysters*
  If the oyster is particularly large, you may want to cut it in half with your fork to make it easier to eat in smaller bites.

- ○ *Savor the Flavors*
  Cooked oysters often have richer flavors due to added ingredients like butter, herbs, and breadcrumbs. Chew slowly so you can enjoy the texture and taste.

6. Proper Condiment Usage

For Raw Oysters

A dash of lemon juice or a few drops of mignonette sauce are classic choices. Cocktail sauce and hot sauce can be used, but keep in mind that raw oysters have a delicate flavor, so use condiments in moderation.

7. Shell Etiquette

○ *Raw Oysters*

After finishing a raw oyster, place the empty shell back on the tray or plate with the cup side down. This indicates to servers which oysters are done.

○ *Cooked Oysters*

Follow the same rule for placing cooked oyster shells face down once you've finished. If the dish came with a sauce or garnish, place the shell neatly on the side.

8. Dining with Grace

○ *Pacing*

Whether raw or cooked, oysters are typically served as an appetizer. Take your time enjoying each one rather than rushing through the plate.

○ *Avoid the Mess*

Eating oysters, especially raw ones, can get messy. Keep your napkin handy to discreetly wipe your mouth and fingers.

○ *Finger Bowls*

Some restaurants may provide finger bowls with lemon-scented water. Use these to gently clean your hands after the meal.

9. Conversation and Enjoyment

○ Oysters require focus, so it's best to pause conversations while you're eating them. Once you've swallowed, you can jump back into the discussion.

- If you're with a group and sharing a platter of oysters, be mindful of taking turns and letting everyone sample a fair amount.

10. Final Thoughts

Whether you're savoring raw oysters in all their briny glory or enjoying a platter of rich, baked oysters, etiquette is all about eating with care and respecting the flavors. Don't rush the experience, and make sure to enjoy the company and conversation as much as the meal itself.

By following these tips, you can confidently tackle both raw and cooked oysters while showing off your dining elegance!

Caviar Etiquette: Enjoying the Luxury with Style

Fish eggs??? Yes, because Caviar is considered a delicacy primarily because of its rarity, labor-intensive production process, and unique flavor. The eggs, or "roe," come from sturgeon, which are not exactly the easiest fish to farm. These elegant fish take years to mature, and their eggs must be harvested and processed with precision.

The whole process can make you feel like you're indulging in something truly special. So, if you've ever wondered why caviar has that "fancy" reputation, now you know! Plus, it's the only time you can say "I'm having eggs" and actually mean it in the most glamorous way possible.

Here are a few key etiquette tips to keep in mind to fully appreciate this delicacy.

1. Tools and Serving

- Traditional etiquette suggests using a mother-of-pearl, bone, or gold spoon. Metal spoons can react with caviar, altering its taste.

- Caviar is best served chilled over ice, but not frozen.

2. How to Eat Caviar

- Caviar is eaten in small amounts, often a spoonful at a time. It's a delicacy meant to be savored, not rushed.

- Let the caviar burst on your tongue to release its flavors. Avoid chewing to preserve its texture.

3. Accompaniments

- *Blini & Toast*
  Small pancakes or toast points are the traditional base for caviar.

- Light accompaniments like crème fraîche, chopped egg, and chives complement caviar without overpowering it.

4. Handling Caviar

- Never Scoop! Avoid scooping large portions. Caviar should be served delicately, as it's both rare and expensive.

- Keep caviar cool but never serve it frozen or warm.

5. Drink Pairings

- Champagne or Vodka? Both are classic choices that enhance the flavor of caviar.

By following these simple guidelines, you'll elevate your caviar experience and enjoy it with true elegance!

A Lesson in Graceful Conversation

Let's return to our friends Rochelle and Markus as they enjoy their meal at the upscale restaurant. As the evening progressed, Deidre, who had been attentive to the finer details of etiquette, noticed Markus's enthusiastic conversation was catching the attention of the nearby tables. She leaned in and whispered, "Markus, you've got the best stories, I think the next table over is enjoying it too!"

Markus jerked back, realizing he had let his passion for storytelling overshadow the atmosphere of the elegant restaurant. He adjusted his demeanor, speaking more softly and with greater poise. As a result, the rest of their meal proceeded gracefully, filled with delightful conversation and laughter, without causing any disruption to other diners.

Their experience highlighted a valuable lesson: it's really important to find the right balance between engaging conversation and maintaining the elegance of the dining environment.

In conclusion, mastering dining gestures and conversations is not about suppressing your personality but about adapting to the context and respecting the comfort of those around you. It's a valuable skill for anyone who appreciates elegance, as it allows you to navigate a wide range of dining scenarios with grace and charm.

Restaurant Etiquette

And there she goes... "Don't you touch it!", my mother said, gritting through her teeth with an order of side eye.

I know at this moment I looked like "deer in headlights" as I took a slow and nervous swallow.

My last jerk flavored meatball had rolled off of my plate and onto the floor.

I think that meatball had something against me because it didn't stop there. It was as if it said "huh, now watch this and stuck its tongue out at me because it continued to roll. Thankfully it dodged the elderly gentleman that was walking back to his seat and finished it's marathon under his spouse's chair.

I look back at my mom to see her darting eyes with a 2nd order of side eye.

"Geesh it's not my fault!" Well...kinda sorta! I was doing way too much talking and using my utensils as a director's wand. She had warned me earlier but what do you expect from a 10 year old? What would you do if your BBQ meatball rolled off of your plate and onto your host's tablecloth or worse her plush white carpet?

Well keep reading and perhaps you'll be able to confidently answer the question by the end of the chapter.

Before you arrive to the restaurant

- Make a reservation

- Review the menu

- Is there a dress code?

- Is there ample parking or do they offer valet services (if so, you'll need a few dollars to tip)

- If you have a seating preference or food allergy/intolerance, be sure to let the restaurant know

Once you arrive
Greet valet attendant and host

Dining alone
Acknowledge the host and confirm your reservation if applicable. "Hello, I'm Christine Carmichael and I have a 5:30 dinner reservation."

OR

Waiting for others

- Wait for the other guests to arrive before proceeding to your table. If after several minutes you're still waiting, you can proceed to your table

- If you are a gentleman and you're dining with a lady and you want to be chivalrous; let your lady walk behind the host or maitre d and then you follow behind her

Coats, umbrellas, briefcases, large bags and purses

- If you are wearing a coat (not a jacket) Ask if there is a coat check. If not you can place your coat over your chair.

- Briefcases, large bags should be checked

- Your purse or handbag should not be placed on the table. You can place it on your lap or behind your back in your chair. If there is an empty chair beside you, then you can place your purse there. Have you seen those cute purse hooks? They are clever little accessories designed to keep your handbag off the floor and away from the table. They are small, portable hooks—usually made of metal or plastic—that fold up neatly when not in use, making them easy to carry in your purse.

To use one, simply unfold the hook and rest the flat, weighted part on the edge of the table. The hook dangles underneath, allowing you to hang your purse securely. It's like giving your handbag its own little seat! These hooks come in a variety of styles—some are sleek and minimalist, while others feature decorative designs or even crystals for a touch of flair.

Not only do they keep your bag clean and within reach, but they're also a fun conversation starter. Avoid placing your purse on the floor, it's considered bad luck in some cultures. If that's not a concern for you, you can place your purse under the table by your feet.

Seating

- If you don't like your table, discreetly ask the host or waiter for another table. There may be some instances where the restaurant may be fully committed with reservations, therefore another table is not possible. You could grin and bear it or inform the host that you had hoped for a quieter table and will have to forgo the reservation for the evening. Kindness is the key here. You may visit in the future so leave correctly.

- Should you pull out the chair? Anyone can do this and it is not relegated to a date setting. I've pulled out the chair for clients, and people who had visible limited mobility, but don't assume the latter, just ask.

- It is so easy to get caught up in a conversation with a friend you haven't seen in awhile but after you've been seated, begin reviewing the menu. If you had the opportunity to see the menu prior, you may know exactly what you would like to order or be prepared to ask the waiter specific questions. Doing so will minimize the waiter's multiple trips to your table to ask for your order. Ultimately, this will expedite your order.

In the world of modern dining, the menu is your gateway to a world of culinary delights. Whether you're dining out at a fancy restaurant, attending a business lunch, or enjoying a casual dinner with friends, understanding how to navigate the menu with finesse is a valuable skill. In this next section, we'll explore the art of decoding menus, making confident selections, and handling special dietary needs with grace.

Review the menu

Save time! By reviewing the menu in advance, you can quickly decide what you want to order when you arrive at the restaurant, which can save you time and help you avoid holding up your dining companions or the waiter. You can take your time to consider the options and make an informed decision about what you want to order. This can help you avoid making a hasty decision or feeling pressured to choose quickly. You can get an idea of the prices of the dishes and plan accordingly. This can help you avoid overspending or feeling surprised by the cost of the meal. You may discover new dishes that you may want to try, if you review the menu in advance. This can enhance your dining experience and help you broaden your culinary horizons.

Menus come in all shapes and sizes, from concise one-pagers to elaborate multi-course affairs. Deciphering them can sometimes feel like solving a culinary puzzle. However, with a few key insights, you can master this crucial aspect of modern dining.

Understanding Menu Sections

Most menus are divided into distinct sections. Familiarize yourself with these sections, which often include appetizers, soups and salads, entrees, and desserts. In some cases, there may be additional sections like specials, side dishes, or wine pairings.

Appetizers

Appetizers are the prelude to your meal. They offer a glimpse into the restaurant's culinary style and can be a delightful way to start your dining experience. Consider sharing appetizers with your fellow diners to explore more of the menu.

Soups and Salads

Soups and salads can be a light and refreshing choice for the start of your meal. They're particularly popular for lunch or as a healthier option.

Entrees

The entree is the main course, and it's where you'll find a diverse range of options. This is where you'll make your primary selection for your meal.

Desserts

The grand finale of any meal, desserts are a sweet indulgence. They offer a wide range of choices, from decadent chocolate creations to refreshing fruit-based options. I've been known to eat less of my main entree or order smaller portions just so I can indulge in dessert. What about you?

Specials

Keep an eye out for daily or seasonal specials. These are often unique creations by the chef and can provide an exciting dining experience. If a special catches your eye, don't hesitate to give it a try. In most cases, your server will inform you of daily specials.

Side Dishes

Many restaurants offer side dishes that can accompany your entree. These can be particularly helpful when customizing your meal.

Ask Questions

Don't hesitate to ask your server for recommendations or clarification on any menu item. They are there to help you make the best choice for your taste.

Dietary Restrictions

If you have dietary restrictions or allergies, make them known to your server. They can guide you toward safe choices and may even suggest modifications to accommodate your needs. Don't hesitate to ask for minor customizations if they suit your preferences. For instance, if you'd like a sauce on the side or prefer your steak cooked a certain way, kindly request it. At the same time, don't be that person that asks for items not on the menu.

Balance Your Meal

When selecting your courses, aim for a balanced meal. Consider a variety in flavors, textures, and portion sizes. For example, if you start with a rich, creamy soup, balance it with a lighter salad or entree.

Portion Size

Be mindful of portion sizes. Some restaurants are known for generous portions, while others focus on smaller, more delicate servings. If you're concerned about portion size, consider sharing dishes or ordering an appetizer as your main course.

Wine and Beverage Pairing

If you're interested in wine or other beverages with your meal, seek advice from your server or sommelier. They can recommend pairings that enhance the flavors of your food.

Gratitude

Always express gratitude to your server for their assistance and service. A simple "thank you" goes a long way.

Avoid messy foods

If you want to make a great impression on a date or at a business luncheon, it's wise to steer clear of messy foods. Why? Because they're not only tricky to eat gracefully but can also take the focus away from the conversation. Imagine trying to twirl a never-ending strand of pasta onto your fork, only to have it dangle out of your mouth like a stubborn guest refusing to leave. As you slurp the last noodle, it smacks your cheek, leaving you with a face full of tomato sauce. Not exactly the picture of elegance or professionalism—and it might just leave a lasting impression for all the wrong reasons.

Placing your order

- Whether this is a relaxing time or you're in a rush, most people don't like to wait. If you have been waiting an unreasonable amount of time for your waiter to greet your table, you may need to excuse yourself and signal to your waiter or another staff member. You could simply say, "We're ready to place our order, thank you!"

- To signal your waiter, first make eye contact. After that you can gently raise your hand and use your hand or your index and middle fingers to beckon them over. But for goodness sake do not use your napkin to wave them down.

- If you are the host, allow your guest to order first. The rule is if you invite someone out to eat, then you are the payee. If you are meeting up with friends, you could say "let's get together for lunch." This infers that we are paying for our own meal even though you initiated the request.

- If you have been invited out and do not expect to pay, it is a good practice to ask, "what do you recommend?" The host could say "I've never eaten here before, the reviews were great, order what you want!" or they may actually suggest an item. Either way, pay attention to the 2 Ps-Price and Portion.

Take your cues from the host

By following the lead of your dining host, you demonstrate respect for their role as the host, and show that you are willing to defer to their expertise and knowledge of the restaurant and its customs. Following the lead of your dining host can help you establish rapport and build a stronger relationship. By showing that you are receptive and responsive to their cues, you can demonstrate your willingness to collaborate and work together effectively. If you are dining at a restaurant that is new to you, your host can help you navigate the menu, the wine list, and any other unfamiliar aspects of the dining experience. This can help you avoid embarrassing or awkward situations, and can help you feel more comfortable and confident. "Ordering whatever you like is not a blank check!" Ask "what do you recommend?" to determine the 2 P's (Price and Portion). If your host or dinner companion orders an entrée at $75.00, order up to that amount but not over. If they order a smaller or delicate serving, do the same. For example, Jason, your host, orders a grilled chicken caesar salad but tells you to order whatever you want. As kind as his gesture is, I would avoid ordering the succulent prime rib steak served with a side of truffle mashed potatoes and seasonal vegetables. Your P & P (price and portion) completely outweighs his order.

Small talk

Watch your jokes! Definitely avoid racial, ethnic and gender jokes. Folks may be offended and not tell you. Avoid topics that could potentially be sensitive or controversial. Political views can be deeply personal and divisive, and can easily escalate into heated discussions or arguments. It's best to steer clear of political topics unless you are absolutely sure that your dining companion shares your views. Religious beliefs can be deeply personal. Money is often a sensitive topic and discussing personal finances or income levels can make people uncomfortable or feel judged. It's best to avoid discussing financial matters unless it is directly related to the business at hand. Discussing personal relationships or family matters can be sensitive or personal, and can make people uncomfortable or feel exposed. It's best to avoid discussing personal relationships or family matters unless it is directly relevant to the business at hand. The best tip here is to refrain asking these questions unless the person you are speaking to brings it up. Be careful not to overshare. Talking about your divorce on a first date may be off putting. Pay attention to the other person's body language to determine if it is ok to continue talking or oversharing. Here's a list of TMIs (too much information)

- **Health Issues:** Sharing detailed updates about a recent surgery and its complications with coworkers during lunch break.

- **Financial Problems:** Disclosing personal debt struggles and difficulties in making rent payments during a casual conversation at a social gathering.

- **Intimate Relationship Details:** Describing in explicit detail one's sexual encounters or preferences during a dinner party with friends.

- **Family Drama:** Venting about a sibling's addiction issues and the resulting family conflicts to a new acquaintance at a networking event.

- **Legal Troubles:** Discussing the intricacies of a recent DUI arrest and pending court case with coworkers during a team meeting.

- **Emotional Trauma:** Sharing traumatic experiences of childhood abuse with acquaintances at a social event without gauging their comfort level or ability to provide support.

- **Personal Hygiene Habits:** Loudly discussing one's recent bout of food poisoning and its gastrointestinal effects in a crowded elevator or at a luncheon

- **Political or Religious Beliefs:** Asserting strong and divisive political opinions during a family dinner, disregarding the differing viewpoints of relatives present.

- **Social Media Oversharing:** Posting hourly updates on social media platforms detailing every mundane aspect of one's day, including intimate relationship quarrels

- **Past Mistakes or Regrets**: Revealing embarrassing details about past romantic encounters, such as cheating on a partner, during a first date with someone new.

What's left?

Current best-selling books, news events, fitness crazes, travel, and sports and Industry-related topics like trends, news, or current events relevant to your industry. These topics can be a great way to start a conversation and show your expertise.

The second option to ease into small talk is by asking others about themselves, their family, work, or hobby. If you know one of your guests or the host is particularly knowledgeable about wines or has wines as a hobby, you might steer conversation to that area.

Can I Order Something Else?

Sending a dish back can be done politely and respectfully. If there's a genuine issue with the dish, like it's undercooked or not what you ordered, politely and discreetly inform your server. Explain the problem calmly and give specific reasons why it's not to your liking. They'll usually be happy to replace it for you. Remember, it's about getting a meal you enjoy, so don't hesitate to speak up if something's not right.

No She Didn't!

One Friday evening, I decided to host a lovely dinner for a few of my close girl-friends at a charming little bistro downtown. The kind of place where the ambiance is as delectable as the food. It was going to be a night of laughter, delicious dishes, and perhaps a bit of bubbly to wash it all down. It had been a while since we all got together.

As we settled into our cozy booth, the waitress approached, menus in hand, and the evening was off to a fabulous start. We all exchanged our orders—everyone seemed thrilled about the chef's special. Except for Mary, who, with a twinkle in her eye, asked, "Could I also get a chicken Alfredo to go? My husband will love it."

Now, let me tell you, Mary is a bit of a jokester with a great sense of humor, so I was curious to see where this one was going. But as the waitress nodded and jotted down the extra entrée, I realized she wasn't kidding. Mary was genuinely ordering a takeout meal on my tab—for her husband!

I didn't know whether to laugh or gasp. Was this a new trend I had missed? When did dinner invitations come with a plus-one for takeout?

Do I act like I didn't hear her order and let her slide? I cleared my throat and said with a smile, "Oh, Mary, I had no idea you were planning to feed the whole household tonight!"

"Oh touché, Christine!"

The other ladies stifled their giggles as they watched the exchange.

Mary, bless her heart, looked completely unbothered. She grinned and replied, "Well, you know how much Jerome loves a good Alfredo. I figured since we were out here, why not?"

Why not? Oh, let me count the reasons! But instead, I decided to use this as a teachable moment—a lesson wrapped in humor. Let me preface here…I would only share this teachable moment with my close girlfriend circle because really the goal is not to offend even when others are offensive. "Mary, you know I love and respect Jerome. He's like a brother, but if you want to bring something back for the family, it's polite to ask first." I winked, softening the lesson with a bit of charm. "Who knows? Maybe I would've insisted we all bring a little something home."

The other ladies hmmmm'd and ahhh'd as they nodded in a "churchy" agreement. Mary was still unbothered but said, "Oh gosh, I didn't think about that. You're right. Next time, I'll ask. But since it's already ordered… I'll just cover the Alfredo?"

We all agreed that was fair, and the rest of the evening went on with our usual blend of humor and good conversation. But from that night forward, "pulling a Mary" became our inside joke for when someone got a little too comfortable at dinner.

So, the lesson here, ladies and gentlemen, is simple: When you're invited to a meal, it's wise to remember that the invitation is for you—and only you—unless otherwise specified. And if you're ever in doubt, just ask! A little courtesy goes a long way, and it saves everyone from "Alfredo embarrassment."

Hygiene

Applying makeup, combing your hair or picking your teeth at the table can be distracting to others. It may be perceived as unhygienic and also be seen as self-absorbed or vain, which can reflect poorly on your professionalism and credibility. Using your knife as a mirror to check your appearance at the dining table is considered impolite and can make others feel uncomfortable. It's best to take care of personal grooming in the restroom to avoid any unpleasant situations or potential embarrassment.

Let's Eat

Here are some dining etiquette tips:

- Begin eating once everyone has been served at your table or directed by the host

- Keep your elbows off the table

- Pass serving dishes to the right

- Always taste your food before adding salt

- If someone asks for salt or pepper, pass them both together

- Chew with your mouth closed

- Cut your food into bite-size pieces at a time

- Don't pick your teeth at the table, instead excuse yourself to the restroom

- If you drop a utensil or your napkin on the floor, leave it there and ask your server for another. It's natural to want to pick it up but it is now considered dirty so you wouldn't want to place it back on the table

- Whatever you put into your mouth should exit the same way—with style. If you're using a utensil to eat, let it do the heavy lifting for removing any

  food, like pits or bones. Eating with your fingers? No problem—just use them to discreetly handle the situation.

- When you're ready to take a sip of your drink, dab your mouth with your napkin first. This will minimize food particle in and around the rim of your glass

- If you need to excuse yourself from the table. Simply say "excuse me, please; I'll be right back" when leaving for the restroom. Leaving without a word or telling everyone where you're going is considered impolite.

- If you need to sneeze or cough at the table, turn away from your guests. Try to avoid using your napkin except in dire situations. If you need to blow your nose, please excuse yourself from the table.

- When life gives you lemons-Don't make lemonade! To avoid accidentally squirting lemon juice in your dinner companion's eye. Pierce the lemon wedge with your fork first, then cover it with your other hand and give it a gentle squeeze. This way, no one gets a surprise lemon bath!

- In some restaurants, you may be presented with a finger bowl after eating your main entree, right before dessert. Usually this is done if your entree was a "finger food" like lobster. The finger bowl is presented on a saucer with a doily underneath of it. The finger bowl consists of warm water and a slice of lemon or a small flower or a sprig of mint. Dip the tips of your fingers, one hand at a time. Dry the tips of your fingers onto your napkin, located in your lap. Once you have dried both fingertips, place the finger bowl to the left of your place setting.

Paying the Bill and Showing Gratitude

Whether you're dining with friends, family, or colleagues, the time to settle the bill eventually arrives. How you handle this moment reflects your etiquette. Let's delve into the nuances of managing the check with tact:

1. *The Art of Offering to Pay*

   If you've been invited by someone else, be prepared to pay your bill unless they have clearly indicated that they are treating you. Offering to pay the bill is a courteous gesture, regardless of your gender or the circumstances. It's a sign of appreciation and gratitude for the meal. If you would like to take care of the entire bill, you can notify the host before your guest arrives. This will ensure that you receive the bill and not your guest.

2. *The Dance of the Check*

   The check dance is the courteous back-and-forth that happens when the bill arrives. One person offers to pay, and the other initially declines. This friendly exchange may go on for a round or two, but ultimately, the one who truly intends to pay should kindly insist and follow through.

3. *Splitting the Bill*

   If dining with a group, discuss bill splitting options beforehand. You can split it evenly, itemize the bill, or use apps to calculate individual contributions. A word of caution - I would not expect a group to be split evenly if everyone doesn't order similar amounts of food. Expecting someone to pay ¼ of a $500.00 bill is unreasonable if they only had a cocktail or a $30.00 salad.

4. *Gratitude for Treating*

   If someone else takes care of the bill, express your gratitude sincerely. A heartfelt "Thank you" acknowledges their gesture.

Expressing Appreciation to Your Host or Server

Gratitude is the hallmark of a gracious diner. Whether you're a guest at a friend's dinner party or dining at a restaurant, expressing your appreciation is thoughtful.

If you're a guest in someone's home, express your thanks to the host for their hospitality. A handwritten note or a follow-up message can be a thoughtful touch.

Server Appreciation & Tipping

In a restaurant, showing appreciation to your server is not only polite but also customary. Acknowledge their service by thanking them, using their name if known, and leaving an appropriate tip. Tipping practices vary by country, but in most places, it's customary to leave a gratuity. Research local tipping customs and follow them respectfully.

Honest Feedback

If you had a remarkable dining experience or encountered any issues, providing feedback to the host or server is appreciated. Be honest and constructive.

Paying the bill and expressing gratitude is the final act in the symphony of dining etiquette. It's a demonstration of appreciation for the meal and hospitality, whether you're dining with friends or at a restaurant. In the next chapter, we'll explore the intricacies of dining etiquette in the digital age, where technology and social media play a significant role in the dining experience.

The Bill

- When reviewing your bill, don't make a production over it. Scan your bill for accuracy and to verify if the service charge is included. Discreetly notify your waiter if there is an error. Whether you've been charged for something that you did not order or conversely, missing an item that you did order

- If service charge is included, this is the tip. The average tip is 15%-20% of the total bill. If you want to leave a tip above the service charge for excellent, or above and beyond service, it will be welcomed!

- In Canada and the US, tipping is customary and usually expected. Every country may have different tipping practices, so do your research before enacting your own custom.

- In countries like Italy, a service charge is neither expected nor mandatory. Many locals will round up. Let's say you pay €1 for a cup of espresso, you may consider rounding up to €1.25. In other instances, leaving the change from a bill is quite acceptable. If you just don't feel right leaving change on the table, a 5-10% tip is more than welcomed.

Leaving the restaurant

After a great meal, which may include dessert and a fresh brewed cup of coffee, we like to relax and take it all in. We now have to give our food time to digest right? It's a good idea to scan the room to see if the restaurant is busy or if you notice other guests waiting to be seated. It is courteous to gather yourself and your guests, and leave the table. You could continue your conversation in the lobby or outside of the restaurant. This will give the wait staff time to clear the table and set up for the next guest. If it's a quiet evening, you can continue to enjoy your company just don't shut down the restaurant (stay until closing).

If you've ever worked in retail, after a long hectic shift and your feet are begging to go home... you can relate!

You finally fold up the last shirt and organize the shelf. You hurriedly look up at your watch and a sigh of relief comes over you because you have minutes before you can "clock out," when a customer casually starts shopping. Your thoughts are, "Ugh excuse me but do you see the time?"

Okay so you might be "that" customer and you might say well it's not 9 pm yet and this is your job!' While this is all true we want to extend courtesy and consideration.

So if you're not going to order another glass of wine or coffee, it's polite to vacate the table!

Tea Etiquette

"Sip, sip, hooray! It's tea time."

I love the fact that more people are drinking tea and really enjoying the benefits of tea.

The health benefits of tea are as refreshing as a cool breeze on a hot day! From boosting immunity to promoting relaxation, tea is truly a treasure trove of wellness.

Let's dive into some of the remarkable health benefits that tea has to offer.

Benefits of Tea

- Tea is packed with antioxidants such as catechins and flavonoids, which have been linked to fight off heart disease and cancer.

- Sipping tea can be super heart-smart, helping to keep your heart in tip-top shape.

- Tea is like a superhero for your immune system, helping you ward off colds, flus and other respiratory infections.

- Need a little help shedding those extra pounds? Tea has your back by revving up your metabolism.

- Feeling a bit bloated? A cup of peppermint or ginger tea can work wonders for your tummy.

- Tea is not just for your body—it's healing for your mind too! The act of sipping tea can be calming and meditative, promoting relaxation and reducing stress levels. Certain teas, such as chamomile and lavender, have natural sedative properties that help calm the nervous system and improve sleep quality.

- Need a brain boost? Tea's caffeine and L-theanine combo can amp up your focus and memory. enhance cognitive function and improve mental alertness. Regular tea consumption has been associated with better memory, focus, and attention span, making it the perfect beverage to fuel your brainpower throughout the day.

- Tea contains minerals like calcium and fluoride, which are essential for maintaining strong and healthy bones. Studies suggest that regular tea consumption may help reduce the risk of osteoporosis and improve bone density, particularly in postmenopausal women who are at higher risk for bone-related conditions.

- Want glowing skin? Drinking tea may help reduce acne, inflammation, and signs of aging, resulting in a clearer, brighter complexion. Some people even use tea topically as a natural remedy for sunburns and skin irritations.

So, whether you prefer a steaming cup of green tea, a soothing mug of chamomile, or a refreshing glass of iced herbal tea, know that each sip is not only a treat for your taste buds but also a boost for your health and wellbeing. Cheers to the many joys and benefits of tea!

Afternoon Tea vs High Tea

What comes to mind when you think of tea?

Elegance? Sophistication? Formality? Traditions? Aromatic? Relaxation?

One common misconception is that afternoon tea and high tea are the same. In reality, they're quite dif-

Alonda West-Johnson,
LaLovely Photography

ferent, with afternoon tea being a lighter, more leisurely affair, and high tea being a heartier meal served later in the day.

Let's compare them:

Afternoon Tea	High Tea
Afternoon tea originated in England during the early 19th century, popularized by Anna, the Duchess of Bedford.	High tea, contrary to popular belief, does not denote a formal or aristocratic affair. Instead, it originated among the working class in Britain during the 18th and 19th centuries.
Traditionally served in the late afternoon, usually between 3:00 PM and 5:00 PM, to bridge the gap between lunch and dinner.	High tea was typically served later in the day, around 5:00 PM to 7:00 PM, after the working day ended.
Afternoon tea typically consists of a light meal comprising tea, sandwiches with various fillings (such as cucumber, egg salad, or smoked salmon), scones with clotted cream and jam, and a selection of pastries or cakes.	Unlike afternoon tea, high tea is more of a substantial meal rather than a light snack. It includes heartier fare such as meats, pies, quiches, savory pastries, eggs, and sometimes even leftovers from the main meal.
Served on a tiered stand, with the sandwiches on the bottom tier, scones in the middle, and sweets on the top tier.	High tea is served at a regular-height dining table, hence the term "high" tea, as opposed to the low tables often used for afternoon tea.
Afternoon tea is considered a social and leisurely affair, often enjoyed in upscale hotels, tea rooms, or private residences.	

In summary, Afternoon tea is a lighter, more elegant affair, served in the late afternoon as a social occasion. High tea, on the other hand, is a heartier meal traditionally enjoyed in the early evening, with a more substantial menu.

Tea Tips
Do's

1. ### Hold the Teacup Properly
   Use your thumb and index finger to hold the handle of the teacup delicately, while gently supporting the bottom with your other fingers. Avoid gripping the cup with all your fingers or holding it with your pinky finger extended, as this is considered outdated and unnecessary.

2. ### Stir Tea Quietly
   When stirring your tea, use a gentle, circular motion with the teaspoon. The go-to is a back-and-forth motion from a 12 o'clock to a 6 o'clock position. Avoid clinking the spoon against the sides of the cup, as this can be disruptive to others.

3. ### Sip Silently
   When taking a sip of tea, do so quietly and without making any noise. Avoid slurping or gulping, as these behaviors are considered impolite and may disrupt the ambiance of the tea gathering.

4. ### Use a Saucer
   Place your teacup on the accompanying saucer when not drinking from it. This helps prevent spills and keeps the table clean. If you are sipping your tea, do not hold the saucer while you are sitting down. Your saucer stays on the table. Additionally, if you need to set your teaspoon down, place it on the saucer rather than leaving it in the cup.

5. ### Stir Tea Properly
   When adding sugar or milk to your tea, stir gently and avoid creating a clanking noise with the spoon. Stir in sugar in a smooth, controlled manner until the desired sweetness or creaminess is achieved.

Don'ts

1. ***Don't Extend Your Pinky***

   Contrary to popular belief, extending your pinky finger while holding a teacup is considered outdated and unnecessary. Keep your pinky finger relaxed and in line with the rest of your hand, rather than sticking it out awkwardly.

2. ***Don't Blow on Hot Tea***

   If your tea is too hot to drink immediately, resist the urge to blow on it to cool it down. Instead, wait a few moments for it to reach a comfortable temperature naturally. Blowing on hot tea can be seen as impolite and may disrupt the surface, causing the tea to become frothy or spill over the rim.

3. ***Don't Dunk Biscuits Loudly***

   If enjoying biscuits or cookies with your tea, avoid dunking them loudly or leaving them in the tea for too long, as this can lead to soggy crumbs in the cup and disrupt the tranquility of the tea-drinking experience.

By following these dos and don'ts of tea drinking etiquette, you can ensure a graceful and enjoyable tea gathering for yourself and your fellow tea enthusiasts.

Hosting your own Tea Party

Tea parties are always delightful because they slow you down to enjoy the ambience, company and food! Whether you're sipping tea in your pajamas with a few close friends or a relaxed gathering or getting " fancied up" for a bridal or baby shower, there's always a bit of magic in every cup. And can we talk about how our little princes and princesses are getting in on the fun? Who knew tea parties would be the hottest trend since juice boxes and nap time? I love it!

There are different types of tea parties:

1. Breakfast Tea

2. Afternoon Tea or Low Tea

3. High Tea

Firstly determine which time frame suits you. Most tea parties that I have attended or hosted have been afternoon tea.

1. Choose a date and time, consider the weekend for optimal attendance

2. Select a theme. Here are some popular ones: Mad Hatter, Mother and Daughter, Victorian Tea, Royal Tea, Children's Tea

3. Select your invitation style, decor, table setting and menu

4. Send formal, written invitations, either by mail or elegant e-invites. Include all details, such as date, time, dress code (e.g., "smart casual" or "garden party chic"), and RSVP instructions.

5. Create your supply list for your tea party.

   ○ Teacup, saucer, tea pot, sugar bowls and cream pots

   ○ Teas-loose leaf or teabags

   ○ Sugar cubes, Clotted Cream, Milk, Lemon

   ○ Jelly

   ○ Strainer

   ○ Napkins

   ○ Dishes, Utensils, Tiered Trays

   ○ Table decor or centerpieces

   ○ Cucumber, egg salad, or smoked salmon for sandwiches

   ○ Pastries, Biscuits, Scones

This is my list for my "Harlem Renaissance Tea Party" for 10 of my closest friends.

Harlem Renaissance Tea Party ☆ ▭ ⌂
File Edit View Insert Format Data Tools Extensions Help

↺ ↻ 🖨 ⬚ 100% ▾ $ % .0̩ .0̩0̩ 123   Defaul... ▾   − 10 +   B I ⊕ A ◈ ⊞

▾ fx

A ▾	B	C
☐	Invitations	vintage 1920s/1930s design, reflecting the Harlem Renaissance theme. Include RSVP details
☐	Tea & Beverage Supplies	Earl Grey, Chamomile, Hibiscus Sugar Cubes, Honey, and Lemon Wedges Cream & Milk Tea Strainers (if using loose-leaf tea) Water Kettle to boil water Teapots for each type of tea
☐	Tableware	Fine China Teacups & Saucers (Vintage or Harlem Renaissance-inspired designs) Teaspoons (gold or silver for an elegant touch) Small Plates for finger foods Tiered Cake Stands for serving sandwiches, pastries, and desserts Serving Platters for food Sugar Bowl and Creamer Set Napkins: Linen or cloth napkins with vintage or Art Deco designs
☐	Food & Serving Items	Finger Sandwiches: Cucumber, smoked salmon, and egg salad sandwiches Scones with clotted cream and jam (grape or blackberry for a Harlem twist) Mini Pastries: Macarons, petit fours, or mini cupcakes Savories: Deviled eggs, mini quiches, or croquettes Fresh Fruit: Grape bunches or fruit skewers for a vibrant touch Desserts: Sweet potato pie bites or chocolate-dipped strawberries
☐	Decorations	Tablecloths & Runners: Black, gold, or burgundy with Art Deco patterns Centerpieces: Feathers, pearls, and candles in vintage-style holders. Consider floral arrangements with deep reds, purples, and greens Place Cards for each guest with Art Deco-style fonts Vintage Posters or Photos: Images of Harlem Renaissance figures like Duke Ellington, Zora Neale Hurston, and Langston Hughes Jazz or Blues Background Music: Billie Holiday, Louis Armstrong, or Ella Fitzgerald for ambiance
☐	Attire & Accessories	Dress Code: Encourage ladies to wear 1920s-style attire—flapper dresses, pearls, feathers, and vintage hats Accessories for the Table: Hand fans, vintage handkerchiefs, or small cloche hats as table decor
☐	Games & Activities	Harlem Renaissance Trivia Cards: Questions about key figures and events from the era Poetry Reading: Invite guests to share or read poetry from Harlem Renaissance poets like Langston Hughes Photo Booth: Set up a corner with vintage props like feather boas, pearls, and hats, along with an Art Deco backdrop
☐	Favors	Personalized Tea Blends: Small bags of loose-leaf tea for guests to take home Vintage-style Compact Mirrors or Feathered Headbands as keepsakes

1. Create a Cozy, Elegant Setting! Whether in a garden, living room, or tea room, create a warm and inviting atmosphere with soft lighting, flowers, and elegant china. Play light background music, like classical or jazz.

2. Set the table

3. Arrange seating with name cards for a personal touch.

4. Start the party by giving a brief introduction to tea etiquette. Discuss how to properly hold the cup, stir tea, and handle utensils. You can provide small cue cards with tea etiquette tips for guests to refer to.

5. **Option 1:** Provide a Tea Selection Experience: Offer a "tea tasting" where guests can smell different teas before choosing. Have a variety of teas from different regions, and consider labeling each one with a description of its origin and flavor notes.

6. The host or hostess should pour the tea and serve guests first, offering milk or lemon based on their preference. Refill teacups only when offered, and always ask the guest if they would like more tea.

7. Mind your manners! Always hold the teacup by the handle; never loop fingers through the handle or grasp the cup with both hands. Stir tea quietly, without clinking the spoon against the cup, and place the spoon on the saucer after stirring. When eating, take small bites and refrain from speaking with your mouth full.

8. As the host, make an effort to speak with each guest and ensure they feel welcome and included.

9. **Option 2: Include Tea Etiquette Games:** Plan games or interactive activities such as "Tea Etiquette Trivia" or have a tea sommelier share interesting facts about the history of tea and etiquette.

10. À bientôt!. End the party with graciousness, thanking each guest for attending. Send guests home with a thoughtful token, such as a personalized tea infuser, a small tin of tea, or a miniature tea set as a reminder of the elegant experience. Consider sending a follow-up thank you note to add a personal and lasting touch

Navigating Global Dining Etiquettes

I magine setting off on a journey across the globe, where every meal is a new adventure and every dining table is a gateway to understanding different cultures. Welcome to the fascinating world of global dining etiquette! Here, mastering the art of eating in diverse settings isn't just about following rules—it's about embracing traditions, savoring unique flavors, and connecting with people in meaningful ways.

Picture yourself in a bustling Tokyo sushi bar, where the precision of every movement is a testament to the deep respect for food and craftsmanship. Or find yourself in a cozy Parisian café, savoring the ritual of a leisurely meal where conversation flows as freely as the wine. Perhaps you're in a vibrant Indian home, where meals are a communal affair, and the rich tapestry of spices tells stories of heritage and hospitality.

Now, imagine yourself in an African village, where the communal sharing of a meal is a cornerstone of social life. In many African cultures, dining is an activity where food is shared from a common bowl, symbolizing unity and togetherness. The rich, flavorful dishes often tell stories of the land and its people, with recipes passed down through generations. Here, dining is more than just eating—it's about celebrating community, hospitality, and tradition.

Every culture brings its own set of dining customs, each one a reflection of its history, values, and social norms. Understanding these practices can turn a simple meal into a memorable experience, full of discoveries and delightful surprises. Whether it's learning to use chopsticks in China, understanding the significance of breaking bread in the Middle East, or navigating the formalities of a British afternoon tea, global dining etiquette is your passport to becoming a more worldly and respectful diner.

So, let's embark on this thrilling adventure together, exploring the nuances and delights of dining around the world. With every bite, we'll uncover new layers of cultural richness, making each meal not just a way to satisfy hunger but a celebration of the diverse ways we come together to share and enjoy food.

The adventurer that I am, I'm always in search of new experiences. I found myself at a grand multicultural gala that celebrated the diverse culinary traditions from around the world. The event was a splendid mosaic of cultures, with attendees coming from diverse corners of the globe. As I mingled with the guests, I overheard an amusing yet insightful conversation between two attendees, let's call them Sam and Maria.

Sam, an international businessman, was accustomed to formal European dining. He had spent many a night savoring exquisite French cuisine and indulging in lavish banquets in Prague. Maria, a vivacious Brazilian, had grown up with boisterous family gatherings filled with laughter and passion.

As they sat down at a long, beautifully adorned table, they discovered they were seated next to each other, Sam to Maria's left. The first course arrived, and Maria immediately dove in, her warm laughter filling the air as she animatedly conversed with the guests to her right.

Sam, on the other hand, adhered to his European dining training, which required him to wait for everyone to be served, then proceed with the meal. As he observed Maria's exuberance, he couldn't help but find the situation amusing. "Such joy in dining," he whispered to me. Initially I wasn't sure if he was snickering or truly enthralled.

Their delightful exchange that evening served as a reminder that understanding global dining etiquettes enriches the dining experience and bridges cultural gaps. You'll discover that, just like Sam and Maria, a touch of humor and a willingness to learn can make navigating diverse dining etiquettes an enlightening and enjoyable experience.

Japanese Dining: A Symphony of Elegance

Picture yourself in a serene Japanese restaurant, sitting in front of a minimalist, impeccably set table. The world of Japanese dining etiquette is a realm of precision and grace.

Here's how to embrace it:

Seating and Posture

When entering a traditional Japanese tatami room, remove your shoes and sit on zabuton cushions. Always maintain a straight, formal posture while sitting. Avoid slouching or sprawling.

Chopstick Etiquette

Handle your chopsticks with care, avoiding rubbing them together, pointing them at others, or sticking them upright in your food. Learn to use them skillfully.

Savoring Sushi

If you're enjoying sushi, dip only the fish, not the rice, into soy sauce. It's a subtle yet significant distinction in Japanese dining.

Tea Ceremony

In a Japanese tea ceremony, follow the host's lead, sipping matcha tea with utmost respect and appreciation. Note that the way you hold and rotate the teacup is part of the ceremony.

Silent Companionship

In traditional Japanese dining, silence is often appreciated. Focus on savoring the flavors and the meal itself. You'll notice that the ambiance and the food become the conversation.

Italian Dining: A Feast for the Senses

Now, let's whisk you away to Italy, a land of vibrant flavors and hearty laughter. Italian dining is a celebration of life, filled with robust dishes and lively conversations.

Here's how to partake in the Italian feast:

Mangia!

In Italy, eating is an exuberant affair. Don't be shy; enjoy the meal with enthusiasm and gusto. It's a gesture of respect to savor the food.

Pizza and Pasta

When indulging in pizza or pasta, it's perfectly acceptable to use your hands. Embrace the simplicity of the cuisine, and relish every bite.

Engaging Conversations

Italian dining tables are often the stage for lively and animated conversations. Join in, share stories, and appreciate the camaraderie.

Ordering Coffee

In Italy, espresso is a popular choice. When ordering coffee, a simple "un caffè" will do. Don't ask for a cappuccino after breakfast; it's considered odd.

Chinese Dining: Tradition Meets Harmony

A Chinese banquet is a treasure trove of flavors and traditions, each dish a reflection of ancient culinary wisdom. Navigating Chinese dining etiquette is an art in itself:

Seating Arrangement

If you're the guest of honor, you'll be seated at the center of the table, facing the entrance. The host will sit to your right. It's crucial to wait for the host to start before you begin eating.

Chopsticks

As with Japanese dining, chopsticks are essential. Handle them with respect, and avoid sticking them upright in the bowl, as it resembles a ritual for the deceased.

Soup and Noodles

When consuming soup or noodles, it's not only acceptable but encouraged to make a slurping sound. It shows appreciation for the meal and the chef's skills.

Offering a Toast

When offering a toast, it's customary to raise your glass with both hands. If you're the younger person, you should raise your glass lower than your elder's glass.

Brazilian Dining: A Carnival of Flavor

In Brazil, dining is a lively celebration of flavors and conviviality. Here's how to join the fiesta with grace:

Feijoada and Caipirinhas

Feijoada, a Brazilian black bean stew, is a beloved dish. Enjoy it with traditional Caipirinhas. Don't rush; it's about the experience.

Meat on a Sword

At a churrascaria, succulent cuts of meat are served on skewers. When you're ready for more, flip your table card from red to green, signaling that you're ready for a meaty feast.

Passionate Conversations

In Brazil, conversations are passionate and filled with laughter. Engage with others, share stories, and immerse yourself in the joy of the gathering.

African Dining: Rich, Bold Diverse Flavors

Table manners and dining etiquette in African countries can vary widely depending on the specific country and cultural background. However, there are some general principles and practices that are commonly observed across many African cultures:

Hand Washing

Always wash your hands before and after the meal. This is especially important if the meal is eaten with hands rather than utensils.

Communal Dining

Many African cultures emphasize communal dining, where food is often served in large platters or bowls placed in the center of the table, and everyone helps themselves. Don't reach across the platters, usually the person closest will serve you. Sharing food is a symbol of hospitality and togetherness.

Respect for Elders

In many African cultures, showing respect for elders is important. This can extend to dining etiquette, such as allowing the elders to start eating first or serving them first. If moving from the dining room to the living room, allow the elders to enter ahead of you.

- *Order of Dining Service.* In some countries or families, the honored guest is served first. After that the oldest male, then the rest of the men, then women, and finally children. Wait until the host has gestured to begin eating or in some scenarios you may be expected to wait until the oldest man has been served and has started.

- *Dining etiquette in a restaurant.* In informal restaurants, you may be seated at a communal table. It's always polite to greet the others at your table but by no means are you obligated to have a conversation.

Eating with Hands

In some African countries and cultures, it's common to eat with hands rather than utensils. This practice often involves using the right hand (the left hand is considered unclean) to scoop up food, particularly when eating dishes like rice or stew. If your host offers you a spoon or fork, hold them in your right hand.

Avoiding Wasting Food

Wasting food is generally frowned upon in African cultures. It's considered polite to take only what you can eat and to finish everything on your plate.

Thanking the Host

It's customary to express gratitude to the host or hostess for the meal. This can be done verbally or through gestures, such as complimenting the food or offering to help with cleanup.

Noises While Eating

In some African cultures, making noises while eating, such as slurping or burping is acceptable and a sign of enjoyment. However, in other cultures, it's impolite and you would be labeled as a villager.

Finishing Your Plate

In many African cultures, finishing your plate is a sign that you enjoyed the meal and appreciate the effort of the cook.

Conversation During Meals

At mealtime, it's all about getting chatty! Talking up a storm helps everyone feel connected and closer. You can discuss anything from family to what's happening in the world. Unlike other cultures, a spirited conversation or debate is welcomed.

Keep in mind that dining etiquette can vary significantly from one African country to another and even within different areas of the same country. It's always a good idea to observe and follow the lead of your hosts or dining companions to ensure that you're respectful of local customs and traditions.

Sam and Maria's International Dinner Adventure

As the evening unfolded at the multicultural gala, Sam and Maria decided to embrace each other's dining customs. They began with an elegant Japanese tea ceremony, observing the precision and respect it entailed. It was an exercise in mindfulness and quiet companionship.

Next, they dined at an Italian restaurant, where Maria introduced Sam to the art of savoring a meal with gusto. As they shared a pizza, their laughter echoed through the restaurant, and Sam found himself enjoying the exuberance of the experience.

In a traditional Chinese restaurant, they navigated the intricate rules of seating arrangement and toasting, raising their glasses with both hands in harmony. Sam's curiosity and Maria's vibrant storytelling brought a unique blend of Chinese traditions and European charm to the table.

Finally, they ended the evening at a lively Brazilian churrascaria. Sam learned the art of enjoying Feijoada, and Maria danced to the rhythm of samba playing in the background. By the end of the night, they had not only embraced each other's dining etiquettes but also forged a remarkable friendship that transcends cultural boundaries.

Exploring global dining etiquettes is a delightful journey that allows you to immerse yourself in different cultures, one bite at a time. As our etiquette consultant learned from Sam and Maria, humor and a willingness to embrace diverse customs can make this experience not only educational but also incredibly enjoyable.

Hosting Your Own Successful Dinner Event

Whether you're planning a sophisticated soirée or a cozy gathering, hosting your own dinner event can be a rewarding experience. However, it's not just about the menu and décor; it's about creating a memorable and enjoyable atmosphere for your guests. From invitations to farewells, we'll explore the art of hosting with impeccable etiquette, ensuring your event is a resounding success.

Hosting an event is not just about providing food and drinks; it's a symphony of graciousness and thoughtfulness. Let's begin with the process from start to finish:

Invitations with Elegance

When sending out invitations, consider the formality of your event. Whether it's a printed card or a digital invitation, ensure it reflects the style of your gathering. Be clear about the date, time, dress code, and RSVP details.

Welcoming Your Guests

As your guests arrive, be at the door to greet them with a warm smile and a genuine welcome. If the guest list is extensive, consider having someone assist you with the greetings.

The Art of the Seating Plan

Depending on the formality of your event, you may opt for assigned seating or let guests choose their seats. Ensure the seating plan encourages mingling and comfortable conversation.

Graceful Dining Etiquette

During the meal, uphold proper dining etiquette, as discussed in previous chapters. Lead by example, and your guests will follow your lead.

Toasts and Expressing Gratitude

Offer a heartfelt toast to thank your guests for their presence. Express your appreciation for their company, and raise a glass to celebrate the occasion. This is usually done when the wine or champagne has been served at the beginning of the meal or just before dessert.

Navigating Dietary Restrictions

In the modern era, dietary restrictions are common. Be considerate of your guests' dietary needs and offer alternative dishes or options that accommodate various preferences.

Au revoir and Gratitude

As the event comes to a close, personally thank each guest for attending. If you're hosting a large event, circulating among your guests and expressing gratitude will leave a lasting impression.

Creating an Enjoyable Atmosphere for Guests

The success of your dinner event isn't solely dependent on the cuisine; it's about the ambiance you create. Here's how to craft an enjoyable atmosphere:

Thoughtful Decor

Decorate your space with a theme that suits the occasion. It could be as simple as fresh flowers or as elaborate as a themed décor. Lighting, music, and table settings all contribute to the ambiance.

Engaging Conversations

Encourage conversations by introducing guests with common interests. Icebreakers and conversation starters can also help people connect more easily.

Timing is Key

Ensure your event has a flow that respects your guests' time. This includes starting and ending the event on schedule and pacing the meal appropriately.

Entertainment

Consider adding an element of entertainment, such as live music, a well-placed game, or a captivating storyteller. Entertainment can elevate the overall experience.

Handling the Unexpected with Poise

Even the most meticulously planned events can encounter unexpected twists. Here's how to handle them gracefully:

Be Adaptive

If something doesn't go as planned, don't panic. Stay composed and adaptive, finding creative solutions to address the issue.

Dietary Emergencies

If a guest reveals a dietary restriction you weren't aware of, handle it discreetly and swiftly. Offer an alternative, if possible, and apologize for any inconvenience.

Unexpected Guests

If someone arrives uninvited, you may want to say. "Oh I didn't expect to see you?" or greet them with a puzzled look! Instead, extend a warm welcome rather than making them feel uncomfortable. If you can accommodate them, do so with grace.

Spills and Accidents

Accidents happen. If a spill occurs or something is accidentally knocked over, address it with humor and grace. Prayerfully there isn't substantial damage or breakage.

Hosting a successful dinner event is an art that combines etiquette, ambiance, and adaptability. Whether you're planning a small, intimate gathering or a grand gala, the key is to create an enjoyable atmosphere and ensure your guests feel appreciated and valued. The next step is to put a date on the calendar and invite some friends over.

Congratulations!

You've successfully navigated a solid introduction to dining etiquette, equipping yourself with the knowledge and skills to dine with confidence, whether you're at a business lunch, a romantic dinner, or a family celebration. Dining etiquette isn't just about knowing which fork to use; it's honoring yourself and others by approaching every dining experience with grace and respect.

Throughout this book, you've seen how preparation and practice are the keys to mastering these skills. By familiarizing yourself with the rules of etiquette, you can carry yourself with poise in any setting. But remember, dining with confidence isn't just a skill—it's a reflection of self-respect and self-worth. That's the essence of "Respect Your Royalty"—embracing your inherent dignity and showing up in every moment as your best self.

As you continue on your journey to empowerment and confidence through everyday etiquette, remember that practice makes excellent. Keep refining your skills, and soon, dining with elegance will feel as natural as breathing. Let every meal, every table setting, and every interaction be an opportunity to honor the royalty within you and inspire others to do the same.

Warmly,

Christine

If you enjoyed *Dining Etiquette Simplified*,
scan the QR code or go to the website below to follow the
author on social media, get updates about her projects and more!

linktr.ee/chriscarmichael

Who doesn't love a challenge?

Challenge 1: The Mismatched Etiquette Dinner

Host a dinner gathering with friends or family where everyone must follow the dining customs of a different culture. For example, one person follows Japanese dining etiquette, another Italian, another Chinese, and so on.

Objective: This challenge encourages you to adapt to diverse dining customs and learn from each other's experiences. It can be both fun and enlightening as you navigate different traditions and enjoy a multicultural feast.

Challenge 2: Chopstick Challenge

Test your chopstick skills by arranging a friendly chopstick challenge with friends or family. Choose a variety of foods that are challenging to pick up, such as small fruits, grains of rice, or slippery noodles.

Objective: This challenge helps you improve your chopstick dexterity while having a good time with others. It's a fun way to enhance your ability to handle utensils gracefully.

Challenge 3: The Polite Tea Gathering

Host a tea party where you and your guests follow the elegant customs of a Japanese tea ceremony. Serve matcha tea and traditional sweets while adhering to the ritualistic aspects of the ceremony.

Objective: This challenge introduces you to the serene and contemplative world of Japanese tea ceremonies. It enhances your awareness of the importance of mindfulness in dining.

Challenge 4: The Samba Sizzle

Invite friends or family to a Brazilian-style barbecue (churrascaria) gathering. Embrace the lively atmosphere, enjoy the flavors of Feijoada, and dance to some Brazilian music.

Objective: This challenge adds a touch of Brazilian flair to your dining experience. It's an opportunity to enjoy a festive atmosphere, explore the vibrant culture, and discover the joy of lively conversation.

Challenge 5: The Silence of the Sushi

Host a sushi night with friends, but introduce a twist - embrace the silence of Japanese dining. Encourage everyone to savor the sushi in a peaceful atmosphere, focusing on the flavors and textures.

Objective: This challenge helps you appreciate the significance of silence in dining, as is often observed in traditional Japanese settings. It's a unique way to heighten your mindfulness while enjoying a delightful meal.

Challenge 6: Language of the Toast

Arrange a dinner gathering where each guest must offer a toast in a different language. Each person will research a common phrase for toasting in their assigned language, such as "Salud" in Spanish or "Santé" in French, and explain the cultural significance behind it.

Objective: This challenge promotes cultural awareness and encourages you to learn the diverse ways people celebrate during meals. It's a really fun exercise that adds a touch of international charm to your dining experience.

Challenge 7: The Salad Fork Shuffle

Arrange a mock fine dining experience at home with friends or family. Set the table with a variety of utensils, including ones that are not commonly used. Challenge your guests to correctly choose the appropriate utensils for each course.

Objective: This challenge tests your knowledge of proper utensil selection and placement while adding an element of fun. It's a hands-on way to practice using different utensils gracefully.

Challenge 8: The Mysterious Mystery Ingredient Dinner

Host a dinner where each guest brings an unusual or unfamiliar ingredient. The challenge is to incorporate these ingredients into a meal while maintaining good manners and appreciation for the diversity of flavors.

Objective: This challenge encourages creativity in the kitchen and the ability to adapt to unexpected culinary situations. It also highlights the importance of being a gracious host or guest.

Challenge 9: The Kitchen Table Diplomacy

Arrange a dinner where you and your guests must act as if you're international diplomats, respecting the customs and etiquette of a diplomatic dinner. This includes seating arrangements, toasting, and navigating polite conversation.

Objective: This challenge reinforces the importance of respecting cultural customs and etiquette, particularly in formal dining settings. It's an enjoyable way to enhance your diplomatic etiquette skills.

Challenge 10: The Silent Dinner

Host a dinner where conversation is limited to non-verbal communication. Encourage guests to express themselves through gestures, facial expressions, and body language while dining.

Objective: This challenge emphasizes the significance of non-verbal cues in dining, such as using eye contact, nodding, and polite gestures. It enhances your awareness of the unspoken elements of communication during a meal.

Attention, Dining Enthusiasts!

G et ready for an exciting opportunity to showcase your dining finesse with our "Dine & Shine" contest! It's your chance to share your skills, gain recognition, and connect with others who love the art of etiquette.

Why Enter?

- **Showcase Your Skills**: Share your participation on social media, tag us, and shine as a champion of elegant dining.

- **Gain Exposure**: Stand a chance to be featured on our platforms and reach like-minded etiquette enthusiasts.

Scan the QR code to upload your video.

Don't miss this chance to "Dine & Shine!"

www.ingramcontent.com/pod-product-compliance
Lightning Source LLC
Chambersburg PA
CBHW070757120626

46557CB00002B/644